Origins of Liberal Dictatorship in Central America

Origins of Liberal Dictatorship in Central America

Guatemala, 1865–1873

Wayne M. Clegern

UNIVERSITY PRESS OF COLORADO

Published by the University Press of Colorado
P.O. Box 849
Niwot, Colorado 80544

10 9 8 7 6 5 4 3 2 1

The University Press of Colorado is a cooperative publishing enterprise supported, in part, by Adams State College, Colorado State University, Fort Lewis College, Mesa State College, Metropolitan State College of Denver, University of Colorado, University of Northern Colorado, University of Southern Colorado, and Western State College of Colorado.

Library of Congress Cataloging-in-Publication Data

Clegern, Wayne M.
  Origins of liberal dictatorship in Central America: Guatemala, 1865–1873 / Wayne M. Clegern.
    p.   cm.
  Includes bibliographical references and index.
  ISBN: 0-87081-317-x
  1. Guatemala — Politics and government — 1821–1945.
  2. Liberalism — Guatemala— History — 19th century.
  3. Conservatism — Guatemala. I. Title
  F1466.45.C595 1994
  320.97281 — dc20
                                                    93-48479
                                                    CIP

The paper used in this publication meets the minimum requirements of the American National Standard for Information Sciences—Permanence of Paper for Printed Library Materials.
ANSI Z39.48-1984

∞

To
Nancy

Contents

Preface

The idea for this work first came to me in the 1960s, when I observed that the interval between conservative and liberal periods in nineteenth-century Guatemala lacked adequate historical treatment. At the time I was doing research on British Honduras, and I realized that the British minister in Guatemala City around 1870 was saying more about local politics than I had seen published. With an eye to the future, I copied most of his political reportage. When I returned to the topic in the 1970s, a search of publications on this brief period renewed my enthusiasm for the British outsider's analysis of events in Guatemala. Unfortunately, there were not enough sources at hand for extended treatment, so I published an article and went on to other things. In 1985, with the help of Thomas Niehaus of the Latin American Library of Tulane University, I obtained microfilm of the *Gaceta de Guatemala* (1863–1871) and the *Boletin oficial* (1871–1873), which together constitute the official journal of the Guatemala government in those years. This material completed the basis of the book.

A number of persons helped in this endeavor. Lee Woodward encouraged me to complete it, and he and Mark Gilderhus read the entire manuscript and offered valuable suggestions. Personnel of the Benson Latin American Library at the University of Texas, Austin, the Bancroft Library at the University of California, Berkeley, and the Biblioteca Nacional in Guatemala City were extremely helpful. My colleagues at Colorado State University deserve thanks for their support. In the course of preparing the manuscript, Susan Jones and Elva Flanigan taught me to use the word processor and printed many copies. In Guatemala, when I was young, V. S. Pinto Juárez helped in various ways, as did Fernando Sánchez and the late J. Joaquín Pardo. More recently, Rigoberto Bran Azmitia gave gracious assistance.

W.M.C.

YUCATAN

EL PETEN

CHIAPAS

BRITISH HONDURAS

Belize

● San Cristóbal

● Comitán

● Chacalá

● Nentón

● Nebaj
● Huehuetenango

● Cobán

Santo Tomás

Omoa

Lago de Izabal

SOCONUSCO

● Tacaná

● Momostenango

● Laguna Seca

● San Marcos ● Totonicapán ● Jilotepeque

Tapachula ●

● Malacatán

● Sololá

Chiquimula ●

HONDURAS

Quetzaltenango ●

● Patzicía

● Arada

Antigua ● ● Palencia

● Guatemala

Retalhuleu ● ● Mazatenango

● Mataquescuintla

● Escuintla

● Jutiapa

Champerico ●

San José ●

● Coatepeque

EL SALVADOR

● San Salvador

Guatemala

Introduction

The revolution that began in Guatemala in March 1871 involved few participants and only about three months, yet it was one of the most significant wars in the history of Central America. It signified a real change in political direction for Guatemala and, it may be argued, for the entire isthmian region. Members of the Guatemalan oligarchy were already moving in the new direction before the revolution, and an important cause of the war was their restiveness. The old regime's demand for loyalty featured the rhetoric of patience, and expressions of impatience were significant in the call for revolution. Debate in the late 1860s about the nature of progress reveals the position of literate Guatemalans within a pattern of thought common to Latin America in the late nineteenth century: Liberalism, "progress," and positivism provided overlapping ideas for leaders who needed to make sense of the country's problems so others would follow them. Yet conservatives in Guatemala thought well of themselves. Except in regard to Mexico, they did not hesitate to criticize larger countries in the region for introducing reforms they perceived to be flawed. Liberal dissidents, in turn, urged their fatherland to abandon archaic concepts, join the march of progress, and catch up with other countries. The political conversation of the late 1860s and early 1870s in Guatemala was an integral part of debates on liberalism being conducted all over the Hispanic world, from Spain to Chile.

What is the significance of those arguments more than a century later? By the 1980s, during the last phase of the cold war, Guatemala had the reputation of being a horror show — a reputation publicly confirmed in 1991 by the Guatemalan president's assertion that he must fight against "the culture of death" in his country.[1] Deadly attacks on Indian villages by the army and assassinations of political dissidents were widespread, even under a Christian evangelical president. Such atrocities had been common since a suspect reform movement ended in 1954. That movement, in turn, had begun in 1944 with the overthrow of the last long-term liberal dictator of Guatemala, Jorge Ubico. The Guatemalan liberal regime that favored such dictators and provided long-standing rationalizations for military atrocities such as those of the 1980s had ruled since 1873, after gaining power in the brief revolution of 1871. Ironically, both this system and its inaugural moment so long ago had envisioned modernization and progress as its goal. But it never acknowledged Guatemala's Indian population as fully empowered citizens.

This regime's enduring political blueprint was sketched during eight years of semiparliamentary government, 1865–1873, when Vicente Cerna (1865–1871) and, after the revolution, Miguel García Granados (1871–1873) served as presidents. In retrospect those years form an interregnum between the two strongest dictatorships of nineteenth-century Central America. The powerful conservative regime of Rafael Carrera (1840–1865) was replaced after the Cerna–García Granados years by the regime of Justo Rufino Barrios (1873–1885), the most powerful liberal of the century. Each of these four succeeding Guatemalan governments was elitist because, among their restrictive aspects, they all excluded the country's Indian majority from political participation.

Public statements from Cerna's regime provide a fascinating selection of the notions expressed by Latin American thinkers of vastly differing political positions in the late nineteenth century. The regime's fear of "foreign ideas," for instance, was expressed in language similar to José Martí's flat assertion that foreign models were irrelevant to mestizo America, with its "Creole personality." Where the Cuban Martí rejected all European models, however, Cerna accepted traditional Spanish institutions uncritically as being fundamental to Creole culture.[2] Martí, a firebrand whose death came in Cuba's final struggle against Spain and after the end of slavery, amounted to a political opposite of Vicente Cerna.

Cerna would have been more comfortable with two other outstanding Cuban intellectuals: Francisco Arango y Parreño, of the earlier generation that fought the Spanish American wars for independence (1810–1825), and José Antonio Saco, a contemporary of Cerna who lived through the Cuban Ten Years War (1868–1878). Arango and Saco represented those liberals in Cuba who resisted any reform that "would shatter the fragile edifice of the slave-based society." They argued that any legitimate reform must rehabilitate the central Spanish power rather than weaken it and that ill-considered reforms such as those presented in the Spanish Constitution of 1812 could only have "the scandalous consequences" of encouraging race war. Their arguments resonate closely with the caution characteristic of Cerna's regime.[3]

In this work I concentrate on Guatemala, but a short reference to its large neighbor Mexico provides useful perspective. An important step in the historic formation of Mexico's system, as in Guatemala's, took place around 1870 in the aftermath of Mexico's devastating wars of reform. Though Guatemala and Mexico differed sharply in national politics, they shared many ideas. It should be noted here that intellectual defense of the epochal regime of Porfirio Díaz (1876–1911) resolved itself into "scientific politics," or "conservative-liberalism," based substantially upon French positivism.[4] Such terminology was not foreign to the Barrios regime in Guatemala.

The intellectual background for the Díaz rationale took form during Mexican debate on President Benito Juárez's 1867 proclamation calling for elections after a decade of civil war and foreign intervention. The proclamation urged "good administration" and "constitutional balance" but also called for adoption of some needed constitutional amendments by popular vote. The Porfirian debate in Mexico eventually embraced the first two pragmatic concepts but would reject popular sovereignty as a dogma "contrary to the principles of science."[5]

The debates on liberalism in Cuba, Guatemala, and Mexico all related to a seminal one in Spain that saw conservative-liberalism represented by the Moderado (Moderate) party. The Moderados' program protected the elite from the *populacho* (that is, from the mob, vulgar democracy, and anarchy) and remained the basis of political debate in Spain from the early 1840s until 1930. The process in Spain paralleled liberal dictatorships of Spanish America in the late nineteenth and early twentieth centuries, indicating that conservative-liberalism, however bizarre it might appear to liberals in non-Latin countries, was somehow fundamental to Hispanic cultures in that historical period.[6]

Dictatorship in both ancient and modern nations has involved the removal of constitutional restraints from executive rule in order to facilitate effective government. The twentieth century has witnessed dictatorships operating under widely different auspices, many with intensely developed ideologies: Ataturk sought modernization of Turkey; Mussolini invented fascism; Hitler established nazism; Stalin claimed Marxism-Leninism; Juan Perón announced the Third Way for Argentina, Getulio Vargas the Novo Estado for Brazil; Saddam Hussein represented Baathism in Iraq; and Khomeini was ayatollah for Shiism in Iran. Thus, dictatorship has appeared historically in diverse forms, some of them surprising. In this work I examine the specific context that spawned a liberal dictatorship in Spanish America.

Notes

1. Scott Norvell, "Serrano grapples with Guatemala's 'culture of death,'" *Times of the Americas* (November 13, 1991), 1, 7.

2. Gordon K. Lewis, *Main Currents in Caribbean Thought: the Historical Evolution of Caribbean Society in Its Ideological Aspects 1492–1900* (Baltimore: Johns Hopkins University Press, 1983), 301–303.

3. Lewis, *Main Currents*, 157

4. Charles A. Hale, *The Transformation of Liberalism in Late Nineteenth-Century Mexico* (Princeton: Princeton University Press, 1989), 20, 251. The Frenchman Auguste Comte (1798–1857) is recognized as founder of the philosophy of positivism. Comte was not an issue in Guatemala in the period treated here, though positivism was often implicit in the discussion. From my reading of Guatemalan documentation, I accept the position of Jesús Julián Amurrio, *El positivismo en Guatemala* (Guatemala: Universidad de San Carlos, 1970), 13, 16–17, 43–44, 63–65, that one reason Comtean positivism was widely accepted in Latin America in the late nineteenth century was that it was preceded by an "autochthonous positivism" in countries from Argentina to Mexico, derived from the general influence of liberalism. However, this view disregards the fact that the United States was even more influenced by liberalism and eventually was attracted to non-Comtean sources of positivism. Probably Latin America was attracted specifically to Comte because he favored the concept of social hierarchy and was able to argue for modernization and science, order and progress, in terms of traditional Hispanic social and political values.

5. Hale, *Transformation*, 72.

6. Raymond Carr, *Spain, 1808–1975*, 2nd ed. (Oxford: Oxford University Press, 1982), Chapters VI–XIV. Also note that the term "conservative-liberalism" was in common usage in the early Third Republic in France (1871–1873), that this had some influence in Mexico, and that events of those years in France were watched closely in Guatemala City.

Rafael Carrera
1840–1865

Vicente Cerna
1865–1871

J. Rufino Barrios
1873–1885

M. García Granados
1871–1873

1

Heralds of Progress

The captain general and president always remembered that he had begun as a guerrilla. Rafael Carrera Turcios (1814–1865), still illiterate when he gained national power, rose to prominence because of his innate talent, his steadfast determination, and the disintegration of politics in Guatemala. During his career of almost thirty years, he lost some battles, particularly early on, but in the end he achieved complete military and political dominance.

In effect, Carrera terminated the Central American Federation and established Guatemala as a separate, independent nation. The federation — an alliance comprising Guatemala, El Salvador, Honduras, Nicaragua, and Costa Rica — had appeared in 1823 at the end of the wars for independence, succeeding the Spanish empire and a short-lived Mexican regime as the governing apparatus of the isthmus. Political struggle ensued for control of the federation. By 1829 the federation's liberal wing had purged the conservative wing, which wanted to preserve much of the colonial legacy, and many prominent conservatives were forced into exile. Now firmly in charge, the liberals enacted a set of reforms beginning in 1829 to modernize the isthmus, abolishing many of the laws and institutions inherited from the Spanish.

Federation is a notoriously difficult form of government, and the Central American version was indeed weak — too weak to settle disputes among its members. The five constituent states reserved most of the power to themselves, resulting in wide disparities in strength. Liberals from El Salvador argued that Guatemala was so much mightier than its neighbors that it would dominate the federation. They proposed to carve a sixth state, Los Altos, out of the western mountain provinces of Guatemala. With this dismemberment, Guatemala would no longer be able to push the others around, and El Salvador, centrally located on the Pacific and home to the capital of the federation, probably would find itself in a position to influence events and policy decisively.

Before independence, the elite in Guatemala City were accustomed to being at the center of government for all Spanish areas of the isthmus and dominating the province of Guatemala, including Los Altos. Now, however, they were split on the question of whether to detach Los Altos. The liberals favored creation of a sixth state, and many of their leaders came from Los Altos districts. Their loyalty was to the federation, which they saw as the *patria grande* of Central America. Essentially, Los Altos liberals were collaborating with El Salvadoran liberals in an effort to divide Guatemala. On the other side of this question were the conservatives. Their loyalty lay with Guatemala rather than with the federation. Conservative resistance to the federation's attempt to detach Los Altos marked the beginning of modern Guatemalan nationalism. It was also fundamental to the rise of Rafael Carrera.

Carrera, however, learned of these broader isthmian politics piecemeal. His leanings were forged out of the hardships of life in rural Guatemala. Born in Guatemala City to humble parents, he moved to the countryside, married at an early age, and was living modestly in the village of Mataquescuintla in 1837. In that year, Guatemala was terrorized by a cholera epidemic that worsened already meager living conditions. Further misery came in the form of the radical legal reforms of the liberal government headed by Dr. Mariano Gálvez. The liberals reintroduced the personal tribute tax, a feature of the old colonial regime that had been eliminated after independence. This tax was a real burden on poor people. Moreover, the liberals' anti-Church policies upset the Indians and ladinos of the rural areas. Thus, the rural population was already alienated from the liberal government when the cholera outbreak occurred. It was easy for the peasantry to accept parish priests' suggestions that the government had poisoned the water and that the plague signified the wrath of God.

These sentiments gave rise to widespread revolutionary fervor. Bands of rebels appeared throughout the mountainous areas of central and eastern Guatemala (*la montaña*). Carrera, believing the government to be oppressive and anti-religious, was one of the insurrectionists. (Always a devout Catholic, he was said to have gained an advantageous marriage as a result of his closeness with the parish priest.) When his neighbors in Mataquescuintla asked him to lead them in revolt in June 1837, his first reaction was pessimistic and negative: If the peasants did not lie low, he felt, they would probably receive greater injuries than those they had already suffered. When pressed, however, he agreed to take charge.

To understand the 1837 rebellion that Carrera commanded, one must glimpse the bitterness of life among the Indian and ladino lower classes in rural Guatemala. Their lot had been hard under the Spaniards, but the three-century-long colonial regime had set aside a place in the social structure for them. The certainties provided by this structure were lost in the wars for independence in the early nineteenth century, and the liberal reforms of the 1830s caused further disruption. To this segment of the population, Carrera represented a return to social stability.[1] Foreign travelers in Guatemala in the late 1830s, most notably U.S. diplomat John L. Stephens, were struck by the Jacobin defiance of the lower classes and their fierce pride in their telluric leader. Stephens tells of the day a troop of *montañeses* entered a town in which he had spent the night. Each ragged soldier confronted individual bystanders, glaring at them and crying "Viva Carrera!" Not replying in kind to each soldier could get a person killed, even if the repetitions grew very tiresome.[2]

As one of his first acts, the new rebel chief issued to the government a set of demands on behalf of his Indian and ladino followers: "first, abolition of the liberals' reform law code; second, protection of persons and property; third, the return from exile of the archbishop; fourth, abolition of the tribute of two pesos per person; fifth, an amnesty allowing return of the conservative expatriates of 1829."[3] These demands were not accepted by the government — indeed, they probably were not even heard by it immediately. Guerrilla uprisings were not Gálvez's chief concern at the moment; his government was also under attack by liberals centered in Los Altos who favored separation. The Los Altos faction, unlike the government, had taken notice of Rafael Carrera, who had shown himself the ablest and most persistent rebel leader in his region. On the point of being defeated by government forces, the opportunistic liberals turned to Carrera for help in overthrowing Gálvez.

He proved to be a highly effective instrument. Entering the capital with 2,500 Indian troops, Carrera and his brother Sotero defeated Galvista general Francisco Morazán in the first week of February 1838. But before the victorious Los Altos liberals could take over the reins of government, they had to pay off their military commander, who had confiscated two thousand government rifles and demanded that his troops be paid 11,000 pesos. He settled for a military command in his home district with the rank of brigadier.[4]

It is ironic that Carrera launched his career by fighting on the side of a liberal faction. Yet in truth he was aligned with no one. Both liberals and conservatives feared Carrera at that time. He was unknown to them and demonstrably crude and powerful. But over time the durability of his talent became evident, and he demonstrated that he was no more brutal than other generals — certainly no worse than the federation's Morazán, who, operating on terrorist principles, had Carrera's father-in-law executed and had his head put on a pike.[5] Carrera won over first the conservatives and then the moderates in Guatemalan politics, but his positions on the issues of Los Altos, federation, and the Church determined that Carrera would never win over the doctrinaire liberals. As his perspective broadened, he flatly opposed the breakup of Guatemala. Thus, he became forever associated with Guatemalan nationalism, a determined foe of liberalism and federation.

When Morazán reoccupied Guatemala City in 1840, Carrera outmaneuvered and outfought him, driving his forces from Guatemala for the last time. The death of Morazán in Costa Rica in 1842 placed Carrera in a new light. With the danger of foreign invasion eased, all parties in Guatemala came to see him more as a threat than as a protector. An almost trackless struggle for power followed, in which Carrera consolidated his base of support; by December 1844, when he was sworn in as chief executive (technically as governor), he was grudgingly recognized as a permanent figure on the political scene.

On March 21, 1847, Carrera committed the act that marked him as the exemplar of separatism in Central America: He decreed that Guatemala was a republic independent from the rest of Central America. Guatemala had actually been separate at least since the expulsion of Morazán in 1840, but now the fact was given formal expression. Perhaps because of this bold move, conspiracies against him intensified. Carrera was not close to either the conservatives or the liberals at this time, and the latter appear to have instigated the two 1848 revolts that forced him into exile. One uprising, led by Serapio Cruz in Los Altos, could only be put down with difficulty, and when José Dolores Nufio mounted a rebellion in Chiquimula, Carrera concluded that the country was ungovernable. He went into exile in Chiapas, Mexico, in August 1848. Once again, the liberals had the upper hand.

Yet in September, facing up to political reality, the liberals declared independence by acclamation in a constituent assembly, reaffirming Carrera's decree by explicit constitutional enactment. This action was precipitated by the arrival in Guatemala City of Francisco Dueñas of El Salvador, whom one writer describes anachronistically as "commisar" for Central American liberal federalism and for El Salvadoran president Doroteo Vasconcelos. Dueñas and the Guatemalan exiles who accompanied him renewed the pressure to make Los Altos a sixth state and pushed for a tripartite union among Los Altos, Guatemala, and El Salvador. But two of the foremost Guatemalan liberals, José Francisco Barrundia and Pedro Molina, now saw that an undivided Guatemala required separate status and turned their backs on federation.

After a year in exile, Carrera returned in response to the continued agitation to make Los Altos the sixth state. The threat of a revolt by highland Indians against such a move paved the way for Carrera's return. The white liberal leaders in Quetzaltenango, capital of Los Altos, were a small minority in a population that was largely Indian. Because the Indian masses still accepted Carrera as their protector, the liberals were powerless to oppose him, and he returned against their wishes to become commander of the army under the conservative president Mariano Paredes. A balance had been struck: Conservatives were convinced that Carrera was necessary to end anarchy in the country, and moderate liberals were persuaded to accept him.

The battle of La Arada in February 1851 consolidated Carrera's power. Demonstrating both tactical and strategic decisiveness, he almost annihilated an invading liberal army of Hondurans and El Salvadorans. For the next fourteen years — that is, until his death in 1865 — Cap. Gen. Rafael Carrera was the most powerful man in Central America. The conservative solution to Guatemala's institutional problems had become irresistible, and most of the institutions introduced by liberal reformers in the earlier federation period were abandoned. By 1854 Carrera's consolidation of power was complete, and he was named *presidente vitalicio* — president for life. His ascension ushered in a conservative renaissance. The Church again directed the educational system; the Consulado de Comercio still controlled both the commercial system and implementation of most public works; the Sociedad Económica de Amigos del País (Economic Society) remained dominant in science and the arts; the district *jefe político* was renamed *corregidor*, as in colonial times; and the colonial Indian law code, which defined Indians as lower-class citizens, was revived — for their own protection.

After the battle of La Arada, Central American military attacks upon Guatemala were rare. Carrera's military reputation was too well established. Most conflicts thereafter occurred when he intervened in El Salvador or Honduras to ensure the establishment of friendly regimes. Indeed, his last

great military test derived from this kind of situation. Carrera had first come
in contact with El Salvadoran general Gerardo Barrios in the mid-1850s
during the National War of the Central American countries against the
U.S. adventurer William Walker. At first their relations were very good,
despite the fact that Barrios was a liberal, and the rise of Barrios to the
presidency of El Salvador in 1859 seemed to promise continuation of good
relations.

The problem was that Barrios's liberal commitments were profound. A
self-taught intellectual, he had traveled in Europe, read constantly, and was
a Francophile. He had been attracted to the positivist philosophy of the
Frenchman Auguste Comte. The reforms he launched in El Salvador
around 1860 indicated that Barrios would be the first of a new kind of liberal
reformer in Central America, sincerely and effectively a liberal dictator.
Because he professed friendship, Carrera merely observed the reform program with suspicion until 1863, when Barrios began to restrict the power
of the clergy. Then Carrera invaded El Salvador.[6]

Carrera's Final Triumph

Gerardo Barrios was a very able propagandist and activist. His reforms
in El Salvador emphasized agricultural development and, after 1861, new
marketing opportunities created by the U.S. Civil War. He did what he
wanted in El Salvador while trying to maneuver away from trouble with
Guatemala. However, by February 1863 Carrera had organized for war.

One of Carrera's most characteristic preparatory measures was to make
certain that his rear was secure; he remembered well the catastrophes of
past Guatemalan governments that tried to fight El Salvador while distracted by the likelihood of an attack from Los Altos. In 1863 his intimi-
dated opponents tried to persuade the dynamic Serapio Cruz, who had
provided so much disruption in 1848, to take the field once more against
Carrera. The captain general's handling of this situation, revealed to him
by his spies, is redolent of his legend.

According to the well-known story, Carrera invited Cruz for an afternoon carriage ride beyond the eastern edge of the city, just the two of them.
Cruz accepted, and eventually they dismounted in a field. Sitting under a
tree, Carrera stated that he would resume the war with El Salvador shortly
and that he would need a united country behind him. He noted the
treasonous propositions that had been put to Cruz and said he could not
afford to let them go forward. Then he opened a case containing two pistols

and suggested that the two of them settle the matter on the spot. Cruz could choose a pistol, Carrera would take the other. Each would grasp the tip of a single scarf and fire at point-blank range, winner take all. If they both were killed, at least their men would not die because of their quarrel. Cruz responded that he had indeed been approached by the conspirators, as Carrera had heard, but that he had agreed to nothing. He offered to accompany Carrera on the campaign in El Salvador and pledged his friendship. They shook hands on it, and Cruz served well in the ensuing campaign.[7]

Carrera was defeated by Barrios's forces at Coatepeque in El Salvador. It was a very hard fight, in which Barrios defended well-entrenched positions. Carrera finally had to back off, and his retreat became disorganized; if Barrios had been able to pursue, it might have been called a rout. By any measure it was a defeat.[8] Carrera retreated to Jutiapa, Guatemala, then returned to Guatemala City to organize yet another assault. He refused to accept the damage to his prestige and pride caused by this loss after so many years of dominance. With his forces reorganized by late spring, Carrera returned to the border and directed guerrilla actions in both El Salvador and Honduras in preparation for renewed invasion of El Salvador. Barrios countered with a Nicaraguan alliance and a Nicaraguan invasion of Honduras, but Carrera was undeterred. In June he invaded, and by late July he had settled into a siege of San Salvador.[9]

Although the U.S. representative in the city saw the Barrios regime as doomed at that point, the struggle went on for three months. It created the classic siege tragedy, a stubborn government putting citizens through horrible privations — consumption of domestic animals, epidemic disease, official hysteria and corruption — with all foreigners endangered by local paranoia. The situation was intensified by the local tradition that, in the many internal wars of Central America, the city of San Salvador never surrendered. This tradition probably explains the Barrios government's unconscionable delay in surrendering. Officials began preparations to leave the city in late August, and a diplomatic mediator led many women and children out under a flag of truce in early October. However, the Barrios government did not capitulate until October 26 (fleeing in the dark), after two weeks of incessant bombardment. Carrera's soldiers were so aroused when they occupied the city four hours after Barrios slipped out that the pillage and disorder were terrible. Carrera could save the U.S. legation only by occupying it as his headquarters. Most of the foreign colony had moved out of the city by October 15 to escape pestilential conditions.[10]

Carrera installed his own candidate, Francisco Dueñas, as president of El Salvador. He remained a few weeks to ensure that the new government was secure, then returned home. His victory address to the troops before leaving made it sufficiently clear that the war had been fought in the name of a conservative (separatist) political ideology. Although Guatemala had not been invaded, Carrera considered liberal federalism to be a continuing source of danger.[11]

It is necessary to understand two things to put Carrera's determined campaign into El Salvador in perspective. First, Guatemala's economy had been growing since 1852, primarily because the country had been at peace and because there had been no significant internal strife. Stability facilitated the startling growth in the production of coffee, which had become the principal export product of Guatemala by 1863. With no war to fight, the Carrera government was able to promote the industry in an orderly way, and most areas of the economy benefited. Barrios's vigorous liberal reforms in El Salvador and his articulate, pan-isthmian, liberal propaganda alarmed Carrera, who remembered only too well the lean years before 1851. Second, the conservative regime that had survived so long under Carrera's protection could only have been alarmed by his defeat at Coatepeque and the immediate drop in his prestige. His subsequent success in the siege of San Salvador, with minimal Guatemalan casualties, made them euphoric with relief. Six months before his fiftieth birthday, their protector was still champion of Central America and apparently had many good years ahead of him. Peace and prosperity for the indefinite future was the real prospect. When he returned to Guatemala, he received something approaching apotheosis.

The celebration was prepared well before Carrera and his army returned and must be seen as the culmination of his remarkable career. On November 25, the *Gaceta de Guatemala* printed a three-day program of festivities to be held upon the heroes' return, with a bullfight as the grand conclusion. For weeks, extensive articles provided admiring analyses of "the War." The *Gaceta* reprinted with some satisfaction a Salvadoran article expressing the ideologically correct view: Progress in El Salvador, as in all Hispanic America, must be slow and sound.[12] There was glory for all: Gold medallions were coined for officers, silver ones for enlisted men, and many promotions were handed out. Four field marshals were named, the most in Guatemalan history: Vicente Cerna, José Víctor Zavala, José Clara Lorenzana, and Serapio Cruz. Each had made a vital contribution at some point in the campaign.[13]

In his message to the new Chamber of Deputies, Carrera accepted the glory in a statement that might be considered either arrogant or resigned:

> Señores Representatives, if I did not understand fully that my person is but an instrument which Providence has designated to achieve what could not be accomplished by other means, it would be prideful to contemplate the important events it has fitted me to direct and the deeds with which my name is united.
>
> It makes twenty five years since, very young and inexperienced in public matters, I found myself in a position to lead the people, who rose in defense of the great conservative principles of all society, which had been unwisely infringed. God, who wished me to serve him in order to realize the work of reparation in our sorely agitated country, wished to give me the triumph. He gave me the energy necessary to command the victorious insurrection and to make the masses of simple but indomitable country people serve the truly civilizing work that I have been able to continue for a quarter century, aided by all good men and always combatted by the impotent audacity of the enemies of order. In that long space of time I have been called three times to defend on the field of battle that most noble of causes, my fatherland, which represented the great social interests. . . . I have seen Guatemala crowned with the laurels of victory. Señores Representatives, we pay the most sincere thanks to Him who directs the destinies of nations great and small, who has visibly protected this nascent Republic and who has selected me as the means to fulfill his wise and mysterious decrees.[14]

Carrera's regime was lauded in Latin American press coverage, which accepted this "instrument of Providence" theory about the war with El Salvador and Honduras. With a flourish, the *Gaceta* published an editorial from *El Mercurio* of Lima, Peru, which bought it all: "Carrera shows himself to be the tutelary genius of Central America. . . . He makes war without resorting to extreme means, [rather using] . . . energy [and] magnanimity. . . . The moderate message of General Carrera to the legislature telling of the campaign, allows one to perceive in the man a great depth of honor and much political tact." The editorialist agreed that Carrera was destined by Providence to teach Hispanic America "an easy way to unite the people," not through artificialities of confederation or employment of "vile intrigue" nor by resort to force of arms but by the simple policy "of observing equity and justice for all, and of treating all as brothers without stirring up the hypocritical cry of unification and fraternity." To illustrate Carrera's moderation, the writer in *El Mercurio* claimed that the government in El Salvador installed by Carrera was in fact pursuing very liberal policies toward public education and elections, the latter being so free that many candidates were running for office.[15]

The year following Carrera's triumph in El Salvador went well for Guatemala, although the campaign left the treasury hard-pressed for funds. Coffee profits continued to rise, and it appeared that cotton production would increase also as a result of the U.S. Civil War and the naval blockade of the Confederacy. Carrera basked in unrestrained public adoration and confidence from both the oligarchy and the people. Spain formally recognized the independence of the Republic of Guatemala. A number of long-delayed civic projects now approached or reached completion, beginning with plans to complete the belltower on the Archepiscopal Cathedral. The site for a seminary to train parish priests, so long desired by Archbishop Paula García Peláez, was dedicated by those formidable pillars of the oligarchy, Bishop Juan José Aycinena and his brother, Pedro, the minister of foreign affairs. The plan for a national bank was authorized, and the safety of travelers on the roads of Guatemala, considered a measure of civilization, improved notably.[16]

In such circumstances, a three-day celebration of the president's birthday in October 1864 was not inappropriate, especially as it coincided with the first anniversary of his victory in El Salvador. The rainy season had ended, and the weather was gorgeous. At the corregidor's invitation, houses and public buildings (Government Palace, Court of Justice, Ayuntamiento, and the Portals of Commerce) around the Plaza Central were adorned with hanging lanterns to illuminate the nighttime festivities. Municipal delegations from around the country greeted the president with local music, dances, and costumes; a military band formed by Indians from Acatenango gained particular attention.[17]

To insiders there was an additional reason for pomp and circumstance to honor the president and display the strength of the government: Carrera's health was failing. During his long public career, the bond of his dominance in public life had been his iron constitution, a veritable fountain of energy. While campaigning in El Salvador in 1863, however, he had suffered uncharacteristic and unexplained attacks of dysentery. In the year that followed, his condition worsened. The poignance of his 1863 message to the Chamber of Deputies, noted above, may have come from his awareness that something was seriously wrong. His message to the chamber at the end of 1864 admitted widespread inadequacies in the prevailing system. "I cannot flatter myself that our standard of living is close to the perfection toward which human society must aspire," he said. "I know very well that the administration of justice, the organization of the army, the system of taxes and contributions and many other branches may demand improvements." These problems derived from "deplorable habits that remain from eras of disturbance and social subversion, habits that unfortunately could be introduced quickly but require many years of patient and laborious effort to be uprooted."[18]

The government as a whole now seemed anxious and gave expression to political philosophies justifying the status quo even while inviting "true progress." A government editorial in December 1864 noted that although war is a calamity, sometimes — as in the previous year's battle against Gerardo Barrios — it is absolutely necessary in order to put down "bastard ambitions" that create obstacles to the peaceful, progressive development of a country. Guatemala had dissidents, but the editor saw them as insignificant; their mere existence demonstrated "the moderate liberty which political opinions enjoy here, as long as they do not try to disturb order." However, in both domestic and foreign policies, he saw Guatemala as enjoying integrated unity of those elements needed to preserve and defend itself. With fascinating logic, the editorialist concluded that, by crushing El Salvador militarily, the Guatemalan government had proven that it was popular at home, contrary to propaganda spread across the isthmus by liberals. The administration had achieved respect for the laws, civil obedience, recognition of merit, and due process in all organs of government. All the things liberals said they wanted to accomplish were being accomplished by the conservative regime. The writer concluded: "*There are no arbitrarities, injustices, nor spoliations; there is not a single will that dominates: it is reason, conviction, and social interest* which presides over the acts of government. In no other way can the secret of *the long duration* of this government, which has become *a phenomenon in the history of the Hispanic American Republics*, be explained than the way we have done it" (emphasis added).[19]

The malignant effects of foreign liberal theories remained a prime theme for Guatemalan conservatives in the 1860s, and the editor hastened to note that a new Spanish-language journal published in New York expressed the political philosophy of the Guatemalan government very well. That philosophy was not reactionary, as some critics of the government insisted, but rather held to the Golden Rule, laissez-faire, and ethnic particularism: "A good English law may be a bad Spanish law, and an excellent law for the United States of America, may give bad results for the rest of the American continent, because laws should conform to the character, to the habits, to the necessities and to the degree of culture of the peoples for whom they are made." The New York editor had presented a thoroughgoing Burkean analysis that asked why reformers must destroy the existing system and expect an untried one to work. For the Guatemalan editor, introduction of the Livingston Codes in 1837 from the United States and the resulting fiasco provided the prime example of the fallacy of radicalism.[20]

In making arguments of this kind, government spokesmen were preparing for the time when they would lack Carrera's sword and prestige. Balance was the political philosophy they emphasized at the end of 1864; the dogma of popular sovereignty desired by some modernists should not be permitted to eliminate the principle of authority. Authoritarian government was lauded for its capacity to slow down reforms so that change could occur at a rate acceptable to the masses.[21]

In early March 1865, Carrera traveled to Escuintla seeking refreshment and relief from his ills. Instead his condition grew worse, and he returned to the capital for what would be his final agony. Official bulletins on Carrera's condition appeared daily from March 18 until his death on April 14. All the pomp Guatemala could muster was mobilized for his state funeral. More than a man had died; the leadership of an oligarchic society had lost its vital link with the masses. The unique role that Carrera had played was best expressed in Article 15 of the Acta Constitutiva of 1854: "General Carrera is . . . the first of our institutions." Guatemala's nearly twelve years of unprecedented peace and prosperity under Carrera best demonstrated his importance. The Jesuit [Father] Telésforo Paúl, who preached the funeral oration, said it best: "What is this sepulchral silence? . . . that strange pain engraved on all faces? . . . the Patria has been orphaned . . . ! This is the cry of pain that has resonated in all corners of the Republic. . . . What do you expect of me today, Señores? A recounting of his remarkable career? . . . No. I proclaim him Defender of Religion."[22]

Considering the contempt liberal historians have heaped on Carrera, it is interesting that this hagiographic description presents him as a man of tact, illiteracy, and Providence; a successful diplomat who controlled distinguished foreigners at his table with "an air of modest grandeur and affable superiority"; a nationalist who told his troops to "serve Guatemala, not me"; and, finally, a stylist who exuded "the majesty of a monarchy, the suaveness of a father." Given the emotional nature of the occasion, this is good evidence of how Carrera's supporters saw him. On another occasion, this kind of audience readily accepted a joint eulogy for Carrera and Abraham Lincoln, who died on the same day.[23]

The machinery of presidential succession, unused since its establishment in 1854, worked smoothly under the direction of Foreign Minister Pedro de Aycinena, the interim executive. He convoked the Chamber of Deputies on May 1 to elect Carrera's successor, and it was done as quickly as formalities allowed. In his last days, Carrera had called in notables of the oligarchy and indicated plainly that his chosen successor should be Field Marshal Vicente Cerna. This general had an excellent military record — he had won battles for Carrera dependably over the years. He had been rather close to Carrera and had no intellectual pretensions (unlike Field Marshal José Víctor Zavala) but displayed a good basic education (unlike Field Marshal Serapio Cruz). The chamber did Carrera's bidding, electing Cerna by a full but bare majority, 28 votes out of 55. The *Gaceta* noted both the excitement of the balloting and the calm with which the news of Cerna's election was received by the public: "[The people] do not want another thing than the conservation of order and the peace which we happily enjoy." Cerna was well known for his long service and *antecedentes*. His good qualifications required little review after his election.[24]

Napoleon III and Bonapartism

In the same issue that told of Cerna's election, the *Gaceta* reported the surrender of Gen. Robert E. Lee at Appomattox. The end of civil war in the United States threw an extremely revealing light on the character and purposes of the Guatemalan regime nurtured by Rafael Carrera. The fratricidal war that had so distracted the northern republic tempted European nations to try the kind of interventions in the Western Hemisphere that the Monroe Doctrine aimed to prevent. The most famous was the puppet empire in Mexico established by Napoleon III of France (1862–1867). Doomed from the start, this regime can be lightly regarded as the famous romantic episode of Maximilian of Hapsburg and his wife, Charlotte of Coburg, playing emperor and empress of Mexico. More soberly, it may be seen as a European imperialist, racist invasion that intensified the suffering of the people of war-torn Mexico. The French intervention was one of those episodes that help to clarify a broad historical panorama.

Louis Napoleon Bonaparte (Napolean III) has been identified as the first of the modern dictators because his empire began with a popular coup d'état and was maintained by the leader's continuing popularity, which depended in turn on his continued success. Coming at the start of a period some have called the era of "heroic capitalism," his successes at home and abroad after the coup of 1851 in France were vast indeed. His concoction of the Mexican empire is revealing precisely because it displayed ambition that plainly transgressed reality.[25]

His Mexican venture was the centerpiece of his plan to make France the leader of all Latin nations, in the economic as well as in the cultural mode. That design saw France as the dominant power in Latin America. Napoleon III was influenced in this conception by the ideologue Michel Chevalier and by the curious intellectual outlook he himself had developed through family background, ambitions, and years in exile. This nephew of Napoleon Bonaparte (Napoleon I), he had excellent tutors provided by his mother, Hortense, the daughter of Josephine Beauharnais, who served as queen of Holland. She stimulated him to learn as much about the world as he could. His family had many contacts with America: his grandmother had been born on Martinique in the Caribbean, and he had cousins who lived in the United States after the Peace of Vienna in 1815. During years in exile resulting from his Bonapartist activism in French politics, Louis Napoleon lived in New York for a few months and adopted England as a second home. Through his own contacts with the government of Nicaragua and through the writings of Chevalier, he became expert on the isthmian canal question long before he took power in France.

Thus, though Napoleon III remains a controversial figure, he now appears less an opportunist and more the inheritor of a famous political name who prepared himself assiduously for the opportunity to lead France. That opportunity finally came in 1848 and crystallized in 1851–1852. His reign (1852–1870) was necessarily filled with great accomplishments, and his "Grand Design for the Americas" was perhaps the most grandiose effort of all. However, it amounted to an interpretation of history and world events that proved in the end to be wrong. Looking at the thought and writings of Chevalier and Louis Napoleon from the 1840s, long before the intervention in Mexico, one finds consistency on three points regarding America: (1) hostility to U.S. expansion; (2) the critical need of governments in Spanish America for stability, which could be provided by transforming them into monarchies; and (3) the improvement of Spanish America through European immigration. Such immigration and political reforms would provide raw materials for Europe and promote American markets for European products.[26]

The concept of French intervention in Mexico in 1862 was expounded by Chevalier in comprehensive terms. France was assured that (1) the Confederate States would be its ally and would guarantee it against attack from the North; (2) Mexico, developed by French efforts and sheltered from attack, would reward all French hopes; and (3) French factories would be assured of getting the supplies they required.[27]

How did the conservative, clerically oriented regime in Guatemala look upon the French intervention and Maximilian's empire? The complexities facing Guatemala 1861–1863 included diplomatic difficulties with the Juárez regime, standard U.S. opposition to European intervention, civil war within the United States, universality of the republican form of government in Spanish America, the fact that French intervention started as a tripartite effort with Spain and Great Britain to collect debts, the political threat of Gerardo Barrios's liberal regime in El Salvador, and the disastrous initial defeat of Carrera at Coatepeque, which forced the long, expensive siege of San Salvador. Thus preoccupied, the Carrera government maintained a cautious but positive attitude toward the French venture. The political principles of personalism represented by Carrera, with a few substitutions, could be found easily in the political theory of Bonapartism. This species of political theory and practice derived from the context of politics in post-revolutionary France:

> Above all, bonapartism espoused an authoritarian democracy.
> . . . A bonapartist rejected both monarchy and republic, entrusting to a Bonaparte the duty of defending him against both, although it should be noted that some forms of republicanism (utopian, fraternal, aiming to abolish class) had much in common with bonapartism and that until the 1830s they were closely allied. . . . Bonapartism recognized the democratic right of the people to determine the form of their government (a right denied by the monarchist) and favored the retention of power in a hereditary dynasty as a guarantee of stability (an idea the republican rejected). Possible abuse of Power by the emperor would be held in check not by the caprices of political parties or the parochial interests of parliamentary deputies but by the sovereign will of the people, expressed through periodic plebiscites. Bonapartism meant representative government, the Bonaparte representing the will and aspirations of the people, with no mediator. Further, it meant . . . [promotion of] social and economic reform while at the same time avoiding the tendency of the Republic to open the door to chaos and violent disorder.[28]

Guatemalan conservatives had a dual interest in the Bonapartism of Napoleon III: order and pan-Latinism, the ideology that pictured France as the leader of rejuvenated Latin nations, including those of Spanish America. The theory of Bonapartism was illustrated and made available in Guatemala during the late 1860s in the writings of Napoleon III himself.

Typical of the Guatemalan government's cautious handling of the political situation was its publication in the *Gaceta* of excerpts from several of Napoleon III's literary works — his book *Extinction of Pauperism*, his speeches, and most notably his *History of Julius Caesar*. The last was the emperor's response to publication of various judgments on Caesar by French historians, writings that constituted thinly veiled attacks on the Second Empire and on Bonapartism. Napoleon III's skillful and eminently favorable judgments on Caesar amounted to vindication of his own regime. Promptly after its publication in France, the work appeared in the Guatemalan *Gaceta*, just two weeks after Carrera's death in April 1865. It seemed almost to be obituary material. The selection showed Bonaparte's familiarity with current historical theory: "Historical truth ought to be no less sacred than that of religion. If precepts of the faith place our soul above the interests of this world, the teachings of history inspire in turn the pursuit of beauty and of justice, and hatred of that which opposes the progress of humanity." To profit from such history as the life of Julius Caesar required rigorous analysis of current political and social changes and, undeterred by "spellbinders who recite details of the lives of public men," a firm understanding of Caesar's political role and of his providential mission. Louis Napoleon argued that the world is ordinarily dominated not by fate but by the complex sum of its own contingencies (*accidentes particulares*): "The object of this work is to prove that when Providence arouses men such as Caesar, Charlemagne and Napoleon, it is to lay out the way for the people, . . . to put the stamp of their genius on a new era, and to accomplish in years the work of centuries. Fortunate the people who understand and follow [such men]!" Those who do not understand, who disown and oppose and then crucify their messiah, are blind and culpable because they do not see that they themselves, by blocking "the definitive triumph of good," are culpable for the delay of progress.[29]

Here, then, was an apologia for the career of the universal historical character, drawn by a prestigious European statesman and used by the conservative regime in Guatemala City to place itself on the side of progress. From this perspective, the work of a providential figure such as Carrera, even if it appeared to some to be "retrograde," really was the quickest route to a better society.

Publication of these excerpts from *Caesar* in the *Gaceta* carried on an interest amply revealed in the previous year. In 1864 Guatemala's elite had shown excitement at the actual arrival in Mexico of the former Austrian archduke Maximilian von Hapsburg, an event that made real the existence of an empire in that country. By the time Maximilian reached Mexico City, pamphlets rationalizing his regime had already been published. The most attractive to Guatemalans was one by E. G. Masseras, entitled *Mexico, the Program of Empire*. For some years Masseras, a French publicist, had made his living in New York as the editor of the French-language newspaper *Courrier des Etats Unis*. He had moved to Mexico City after the French expeditionary force occupied it and published the pamphlet before Maximilian arrived. This document, written in French, so impressed Guatemalan government officials that they translated it into Spanish and published it in Guatemala City amid the excitement accompanying news of Maximilian's arrival in Mexico.

The pamphlet featured a theme extremely attractive to the ruling class of Guatemala: Great trees grow slowly. Masseras asserted that this law of gradual development was universal, applying equally to the moral and the material order, public and private life, communities and individuals. To create something stronger, greater, and more durable required slow, hard preparatory work, great sacrifices, and some anxiety. The metaphor of gestation, birth, and slow, anguished growth toward maturity was basic to Masseras's analysis. He interpreted the miseries and errors of Mexican history in this light and concluded that the empire would save Mexico.

To assure progress and "fruitfulness," preparatory work had to be measured and intelligent, and delays and challenges had to be endured with patient confidence in the future. "To force the pace exaggeratedly, to change direction each instant on the pretext of speeding it, to try to substitute the use of violence for the action of time, is to prepare an inevitable abortion," he asserted. "The fatal error Mexico committed, which has now to be corrected, has been precisely that of . . . failing to persevere and of mistaking mere change for progress." In elegant abstraction, Masseras described political and social degradations that had occurred in Mexico during the age of Santa Anna. In such a situation the corrective element could only come from outside the country, he argued; domestic solutions would merely reignite the battles of the past. Thus, the outside solution had to be "a definitive regime," because permanence would stifle the ambitious agitation fomented against all short-term power. "The Empire, then, brings salvation to Mexico on the only conditions under which that salvation is possible."[30]

Masseras pictured the empire as a vehicle for a new current of ideas in Mexico and in Spanish America generally. Though he did not use the term, Masseras referred to pan-Latinism: "The foresightful character (*genio*) and energetic hand that have reestablished the union of the Latin race in Europe, have wished to . . . elevate that same race in the new world to a corresponding rank." The first requirement was to halt Spanish America's decline by eliminating anarchy. Mexico was to be the focal point for generating a new life in the region. "I have here the secret of the intervention in Mexico and creation of the empire. . . . Far from thinking to enslave Mexico, France has wished only to place it in a position to preside over the great work of regenerating Spanish America."

Independence for Mexico had dawned brightly in the 1820s, at which moment it might have been envied by the most favored of countries. "It had within itself the germs and elements of all kinds of prosperity and greatness," Masseras wrote. "Institutions which the government of the old metropolis had left it did not need more than gradual, intelligent modifications to give impulse to agriculture, industry, commerce, and shipping, which would have made Mexico compete effectively even with the United States." The newly independent nation's natural resources had made its public credit seem inexhaustible. "Its name alone was synonymous in the eyes of the world with limitless wealth and prosperity."

Acidly commenting on the loss of half of Mexican territory to the rapacious Anglo-Saxons to the north, Masseras explained (with Gallic logic?) how Mexico had never really been a republic and how the empire of Maximilian would provide the essence of a republic: "Can one describe sincerely as a Republic that perpetual anarchy in which a regularly elected executive recognized by the entire country, or allowed by his rivals to complete a normal term of office can scarcely be found? . . . No. The Republic is not that capricious succession of chiefs who proclaimed themselves, elevated to office by phony elections which condemn them to be instruments of a party instead of administrators for the whole public. Mexico has not known more than the name and the shadow of a Republic."

Thus, Masseras contended, inauguration of the empire could not steal what Mexico never had. "Better said, the Empire brings in fact that which constitutes the essence of the Republic in the pure and true meaning of the word, and that which the so-called Republic under which Mexico has lived so far has not been able to give it." True liberty is order, "that which each citizen finds under the shield of a single law, precise and defined, equal for all, and that all will be certain to find unchanged each day." Once such liberty is assured, each citizen participates in public questions, first by discussion, then through national representation. "We submit ourselves to strict truth, affirming that the Empire will bring the country that which the Republic never has given, not only from the social point of view but from the political. . . . Napoleon III has given to the word empire a new meaning which no one can take away from it." Formerly it had carried the idea of absolute, unfettered government, but in his policy it signified "the intimate alliance of the democratic and progressive principle of modern times, with the conservative principle of an established government." The French example of the previous dozen years was a precedent "destined to be converted by moral power, into a general . . . rule for the entire world."

If some were to demand either blind re-establishment or complete destruction of past arrangements, Masseras warned, they would soon find that "moderation does not exclude firmness" in a government resolved to seek the true general interest. The work of fusion required a long view that had been lost in Mexico. The empire would reveal a harmony among classes that would prevent destabilizing partisanship. In Mexico, institutions such as the clergy, courts, and army had fallen into a state of permanent antagonism, "a vicious circle from which they could not escape." No party seemed able to re-establish political equilibrium. That would change under Napoleon: "The Empire will place each of the great corporations of the State in its proper sphere, lay out again the forgotten limits, and in compensation guarantee them their inviolability. . . . Thus assured their reciprocal independence under the hand of the Chief of State, they will be what they ought to be: the guardians of Religion, of Law, and of Order, and the united protectors of society." With each institution guaranteed its appropriate dominion, those who were previously disillusioned would be surprised by how much they gained in real power and prestige.

The legislature's proper role presented a different problem. Masseras argued that lawmakers must break away from the old bad habits, sterile controversies, and special interests that warped public dialogue. His argument described unfettered parliamentary debate as mere license for the worst side of human nature. Instead he seemed to favor a *corps legislatif* such as then existed in France.[31] Though it appeared unwise to open a congressional arena where passions and rancor could lead to anarchy, the citizenry did need training in the skills of public expression. Responsible freedom of speech and of the press should be exercised as a form of public education. Circumstances of the new regime seemed to indicate a political program with "many analogies" to that of Napoleon III in France. Napoleon took the mass of the nation itself as his base of support and separated governing forces into their respective spheres, concentrating their efforts later into common action. He reserved to the sovereign ample initiative, giving him the power to extend public liberties and popular prerogatives as a prudently graduated counterpoise.

As to persons who would be chosen to work with the sovereign, "the essential quality that is sought will be the rectitude of their intentions and

great probity, rather than an eminent talent. . . . Political antecedents . . .
will be unimportant in an order of things which seeks a complete break
with the past." After the chief of state had an opportunity to study the
situation and persons available, he would know how to select those who
would help him in his difficult mission. There would be "new labor that
demands new men."

Masseras insisted that his repeated use of the expression "classes that
govern" ought not "be interpreted in the sense . . . of aristocratic distinction.
It is no more than a simple collective designation under which we have
wished to include the center of the constituted bodies that support the
national administration in either a monarchical or a republican political
organization." In a society's own interest, the government should be composed of members of a high rank on the social scale, "but only within reason
and within the limits of the functions which they exercise and not in
consequence of any privilege especially conceded analogous to those which
may distinguish a noble class." By providing order and equity, the empire
would broaden opportunities for the masses and mobilize them for the
nation. A series of reforms in all branches of administration and political
economy would effect a moral and material transformation of the country.
Democracy in the empire would provide the device.

Finally, the threat of U.S. intervention was converted into an asset.
"Who can say that there is not something providential in the coincidence
that places Mexico precisely on the road to a regeneration that can scarcely
be imagined in the same hour that the great American union is destroyed
in the conflict of a great civil war?" Masseras asked. What part might the
Mexican empire play in the distribution of "that colossal prosperity" by
which the United States had gained the admiration of the world and which
it now had lost, probably without hope of recovery? "To those who accuse
us of evoking impossible dreams, we respond by exhibiting the France of
1864 beside that of 1851. In her they will see what some well-employed
years in the life of a nation can do." The Guatemalan conservatives
concurred, pointing out repeatedly what the identical well-employed years
under Carrera had done for their country, and they could relate easily to
what Masseras had to say about "practical democracy."[32]

The attractiveness of Mexican events in the eyes of the Guatemalan
elite was related to the general appeal of Napoleon III's program of pan-
Latinism in Spanish America. By the 1860s the world had reached a
historical juncture where social results of the Industrial Revolution im-
pacted political forms in a decisive way; the emperor of the French, indeed
the entire Western Hemisphere, demonstrated as much. Napoleon III

grasped early several elements of the new era into which European civilization was moving: that the masses were awakening, becoming better informed; that the pattern of order derived increasingly from industrial society, with nationalism as its ideology; and that the new technology had the global capacity to create huge new accumulations of capital. But he erred in predicting the political form of the future. Nationalism indeed was in that future, but monarchy was not.

The Cerna Conservatives

Napoleon III was an accomplished and articulate politician whose successes in the 1850s and 1860s strengthened the plausibility of his theories, providing a model of success for other European rulers of his era. In Latin America he enjoyed prestige among many conservatives before his failure in Mexico. In Guatemala his popularity manifested itself in such ephemeral matters as grooming styles among the elite. The prominent press coverage given to the comments of the French chargé at state banquets and the printing of an occasional speech by Napoleon III himself were are also suggestive. Most notable, however, was the convergence of Guatemalan official political sentiments with those of Bonapartism.

When the situation of Maximilian deteriorated in 1866–1867, Guatemalan attention swung sharply from Napoleon III to the resurgent, hostile Juárez government in Mexico. By 1867 the *Gaceta* was not only cautious where Mexico was concerned but reacted in a clearly defensive mode. It expressed alarm that a newspaper in the neighboring state of Chiapas reported Guatemalans occupying Mexican territory; it appealed in aristocratic tones for maintenance of peace and the status quo in all of Central America. The surrender of Maximilian to forces of Juárez brought the pious hope that peace would come to war-torn Mexico. The same sentiments were expressed at news of the execution of Maximilian. A European account excoriating the execution was reprinted in the *Gaceta* but was retracted in the next issue with the editor's abject comment that its printing was an oversight and did not represent the editorial view of the journal.[33]

Spanish and Portuguese America had received a never-ending stream of political ideas from Europe. After they achieved political independence, a particular problem for Latin Americans was to select from the spectrum of European ideas those that really would assist in developing the kind of society they wanted. The ultimate selection — that is, the ideology that was most widely adopted and most influential by the 1870s — was the positivism of Auguste Comte. This was a republican scheme in its Spanish American (Littréist) form. The pan-Latinism of Napoleon III, which favored monarchy in Mexico at least, was a notable ideological rival until the failure of the French-Mexican experiment in 1867. Indeed, the prominence of positivism in the program of Benito Juárez's reform regime made the empire of Maximilian a showcase for that ideological rivalry. The execution of Maximilian on Querétaro's Hill of the Bells in 1867 was the death knell for monarchist theory in Spanish America and foreshadowed its end in Brazil in 1889.[34]

The major role played by the Roman Catholic Church in the French venture in Mexico stirred interest among the Guatemalan elite. Proportionally, the Church had more influence on government policy in Guatemala than in France, but the governments of both could be characterized as defenders of the Vatican. The difference in context, however, was dramatic. In Guatemala the Church was organized along conservative Spanish lines, dominating the intellectual and institutional atmosphere almost completely. However, the only instrument it could find to save that society from anarchy or from the equally "destructive" changes of modernization had been the violent but devout Rafael Carrera. In France the Church had many more intellectual and institutional challengers but also more diverse champions — it was relatively enlightened and tolerant. Napoleon III, the master politician, saw the Church as useful, and in his cynicism he protected it while controlling it.

Although Comte's positivism was republican and ostentatiously scientific, its call for the retention of social hierarchy was vital to its acceptance in Latin America. It saw society as ruled by natural leaders. Because the presuppositions of Spanish American society were fundamentally oligarchic, positivism became the most attractive of European modernizing theories to Latin American elites. Latin American leadership was socially conservative in the nineteenth century, even elements that proposed notable reform in the social structure, such as the Juárez generation in Mexico or the Liberal Party in the Central American Federation. The common idea that allowed positivists and monarchists alike to advocate change and stability simultaneously was *progress*. This word, so rich in symbolism, served diverse points of view. By advocating it monarchists could retain their favorable class structures in the face of radical material development. Positivists could and did identify it in an abbreviation of the motto provided by Comte: "Order and Progress."

During and after the rule of Rafael Carrera, a quasi-monarch, conservatives in Guatemala spoke passionately for "true progress." They understood clearly that material development was not only desirable but necessary in the world they faced, yet they hoped to avoid radical social change — a desire they attributed to liberals such as Gerardo Barrios. They considered a number of the institutions inherited from Spain and resurrected by Carrera's counterrevolution to be necessary to civilization. Liberal leaders in Guatemala thought otherwise. They maintained that the institutional pattern bequeathed by Spain, particularly the position of the Church, was an obstacle to progress. An atmosphere increasingly favorable to positivism strengthened the liberals' position in this regard.

Oligarchy means, literally, "rule by the few." The word can serve as a generic term for an elite, an aristocracy, or any other small class that rules. The oligarchy that ruled Guatemala, as compared to those of other Spanish American countries at the time of independence in the 1820s, was unusually well integrated. Two well-known circumstances contributed to this cohesion: (1) Guatemala City had been the governing seat of the isthmian provinces and thus the site of the ruling institutions of the captaincy general of Guatemala; and (2) the family network of the Marquis of Aycinena, the only titled nobleman in the region, resided there. Everywhere in Spanish America, the oligarchy tended to be organized on family structure. In the province of El Salvador, for instance, "the fourteen families" were supposed to compose it. Some said that in Guatemala the power structure revolved around only four family names: Aycinena, Batres, Pavón, and Piñol. These families and their close allies were so intermarried as to be known simply as "la familia." The total number of persons who could claim peripheral membership in the oligarchy by reason of education, wealth, or appointment was relatively small. The career and failure of the Central American Federation and especially the conservative peasant movement that overthrew it extended membership to some ladinos (people of mixed Indian-white ancestry who took on European culture). Aside from European immigrants, most new members in the 1840s and 1850s were military men who participated peripherally in a social sense.

The turnover of generations in an orderly way is vital to such an arrangement, and it should be noted that around 1865 a significant number of individuals important to the oligarchy died. Carrera himself, who would have been a classic peripheral member of the elite group except for the unique fact that he dominated it, died in the spring of 1865. Preceding him in death by two months was Dr. Juan José (the Marquis of) Aycinena, bishop of Trajanópolis, who had chosen somewhat late, after qualifying with distinction in both civil and canon law, to become a priest. Another bishop, José María Barrutia (1864), and the longtime archbishop, Francisco de Paula García Peláez (1866), joined the marquis in death. In addition to the passing of these men, who had provided leadership in a government with strong theocratic leanings, a death of symbolic significance occurred in Cuba in 1866: Mariano Beltranena, last living signer of Central America's Declaration of Independence, passed on. Lesser lights such as Father Matías Córdova, a founder of the Economic Society, were lost at the same time.[35] The generation disappearing with Carrera was the one that had seized independence from Spain and Mexico, survived the purges by federation liberals, and in turn purged the liberals. Now the torch was being passed from these survivors to a new generation.

The man who would preside over this generational changing of the guard was Field Marshal Vicente Cerna, whom the dying Carrera had presented to the establishment as his chosen successor. The succession was smooth, although Cerna received a stiff challenge. Balloting occurred on May 3 in a general assembly established by requirement of the Acta Constitutiva of 1854 as a committee of the whole of the Chamber of Representatives. Don Pedro de Aycinena, minister for foreign affairs and acting president, had convened the general assembly, charging it to do its civic duty: "Relying always on the aid of Divine Providence and on the patriotism of Guatemalans, we should expect, Señores, that the country will not retrocede nor lose the good name which it has acquired."[36] Cerna won on the second ballot by a bare majority of 28 votes to 25 for Councillor of State Manuel Francisco González and 2 for Field Marshal José Víctor Zavala. Two representatives refused to sign the final acts certifying Cerna's election — Miguel García Granados and Marcos Dardón.

The *Gaceta* described the assembly's gallery as full, grave, and tense throughout the voting but claimed the victory of Cerna brought jubilation, both in the hall and in the street. The calm and moderation of the election and the public's joyful reception of the results indicated that, indeed, it was more concerned about the preservation of peace and order than about civil liberties and reform. Cerna was noted for his long service and good background and "thus his good qualifications are well-known."[37]

It was an altogether establishmentarian performance. Transition was aided greatly by voluntary loans to the provisional government from prominent citizens. The *Gaceta* noted proudly that the government had refused to demand forced loans, a remedy often used in preceding decades. After elaborate ceremonies informing Cerna of his election, which included a delegation from the assembly traveling to his home in Chiquimula to give him the official result, and his triumphal return to the capital, the new president was inaugurated on May 24 and issued a manifesto to the nation. Designed to inspire confidence, it expressed no new idea. Rather, Cerna pronounced that "citizens will enjoy the just and prudent liberty which they have always obtained through our laws and customs." He insisted that the energetic political thought that had drawn Guatemala from chaos and ruin twenty-six years before would continue to inspire the government.[38]

Closing of the conservative ranks was demonstrated at a banquet several days earlier by the president-elect for about fifty luminaries. In that moment of high tide for Maximilian's neighboring regime, the French chargé occupied an important place at the banquet. He offered a lengthy toast that honored Cerna for defending and preserving the concept bequeathed to Guatemala by Carrera, the nation's glorious historical leader. "That concept . . . is a guarantee . . . to conserve the social edifice of peace, order, religion, and independence, raised in the midst of the greatest difficulties by [a] truly extraordinary man." The chargé then toasted Cerna and his government for continuity of policy and reminded all Guatemalans that the representative of Napoleon III was there to assist and support them in any way that he could.[39]

In his first weeks as president, Cerna pursued public symbolism vigorously. To maximize personal prestige gained in the campaign of 1863 against El Salvador and Honduras, on June 12 he and his minister of war distributed awards (the Cross of Honor) to 344 personnel of all ranks. Amnesty for political exiles was declared to demonstrate the government's confidence, but it was not quite complete; individuals would be required to obtain permission in the form of an appropriate passport before returning to Guatemala. Spokesmen asserted that although Guatemala had been accused of being "absolutist and arbitrary" in such matters, its record was actually better than that of certain other countries that boasted constantly of their legality. Noted the *Gaceta*, "Here, there are hardly five or six persons exiled from their country for political reasons; and those not precisely for their political opinions, which are tolerated when they do not trespass the bounds of the law, but for acts by which they have attempted more or less directly to disturb the public order."[40] According to the writer, the recent Carrera regime needed no defense against those who asserted that it had been *poco legal* (hardly legal). One needed merely to state the fact that at the end of the regime, "Guatemala . . . has scarcely a half dozen political exiles. Can you name and say as much for other countries that are said to be more liberal than ours?"[41]

On September 15, 1865, commemorating the forty-fourth anniversary of independence from Spain, the Cerna government published an essay that constitutes perhaps the most perfect statement of its philosophical conservatism. It ignored indigenous Indians as political beings, affirmed Spain as the mother country, and recognized European superiority.

> We shall not attack [Guatemala's] memory by enumerating our past mistakes and misfortunes: these are reserved to the judgment of history and to the impartial criterion of the generations that succeed us. Even less shall we permit the committing of any unmerited offense to the memory of the valiant conquistadors and ancient governments to whom we owe our present civilization. They are also our fathers, and obeying the tendencies and preoccupations of their time, they did no more than subject themselves to a superior force which it would have been vain to resist.
>
> Commemorating today the great and necessary fact of Guatemalan independence, we do it without hatred or reservations: we believe that the hour of emancipation arrived through force of circumstances, and that independence was proclaimed as an absolute necessity, but without breaking the natural ties that existed. Time perhaps has strengthened those ties; and the old mother country, conceding to us that which is our right, has now recognized our independence. So it is our duty, as it has been, to conserve worthily that honorable position, learning from the lessons of experience and from salutary examples which the history of cultured peoples offers us daily.
>
> *The epoch is past when we were able,* by means of our ardent and patriotic desires, *to hallucinate with imaginary importance and greatness: today we know our relative worth;* and this places us without any doubt in a position to judge events with greater certainty. By means of this knowledge *we shall not claim more than is appropriate to us,* nor shall we defy insensitively a force superior to our elements and resources (emphasis added).[42]

Having sketched so modest an interpretation of history, the government presented in the following month an analysis of its immediate political concerns, asserting that the present regime had a good record of quietly and slowly solving the problems of society both before and after the death of General Carrera. Inside and outside Central America it was recognized that Guatemalans had so learned the necessity of peace "that today it would be perhaps a vain enterprise . . . to try to divert the people from the path of positive wellbeing on which they travel by deluding them with lying promises of future prosperity. The worthy Chief of the Republic . . . labors unceasingly to perfect and carry forward the work of his illustrious predecessor." Cerna wanted to aggrandize Guatemala by reasonable and regular means. Consequently, he was seen to be decisive in practical matters, carefully avoiding deceptive and dangerous abstractions. But he sought intelligent cooperation with all enlightened Guatemalans; he wished to perfect the ruling institutions; he respected the customs and traditions of local communities and promoted the general prosperity of all as was feasible.

Cerna was certain to carry forward the "wholesome reaction" of 1839. Clearly, said the editor, much remained to be done to eliminate bad habits acquired during the federation period and to stimulate national development on the basis of "good principles to which Guatemala owes the happy situation in which it finds itself. Proceeding in this manner, we should not fear that those [principles] might perish in the clash with contrary ideas." Public confusion could always be eliminated by "people who, like ourselves, still conserve in large part . . . *the habits of regularity and order that the colonial government established*" (emphasis added).

The editor claimed that those with ulterior motives, those who believed that the system of the liberal-federation period could be revived, were mistaken. Only a sudden change in social conditions could cause such a revival. The public had learned from the turbulence in Guatemala and in Latin America generally "to appreciate systems and men by the positive effect of deeds, and not by the attractiveness of their forms, still less by pompous and sonorous words." Having asserted that the people were now immune to false liberal prophets, the editor literally prayed that this was true:

> May we live tranquil, then, trying always, as we have till now, to impel public sentiment toward order and peace; may we take care to make effective in their natural meaning the prescriptions of the laws and the authorities; may we not debase power with false interpretations of its decrees and resolutions, nor may we manifest an extreme susceptibility in all that which refers to the general good; may we prefer the truth to formulas, and may we face with courage the responsibility for the consequences of our own acts, without comparing them to others. . . . Thus . . . we may have even more well-founded probability that the Republic will continue being prosperous and happy.[43]

A good symbol of the Cerna regime's idea of progress was a new museum for the Economic Society. The Economic Society was one of those Spanish institutions revived after independence, but, unlike other such institutional holdovers, it was not controversial: Both conservatives and liberals saw it as useful. Its basic purpose was to promote useful knowledge, and its membership was limited only by literacy. The museum was inaugurated for

New Year's 1866 with elaborate ceremony and speeches indicative of the philosophy of the regime. A lawyer-accountant, Rafael Machado, spoke in expansive and completely conciliatory terms of the purposes of the museum and those who founded it. He saw museums as vehicles of knowledge and progress. This one had been authorized by governmental decree almost thirty-five years before, in October 1831, but not until the early 1850s had officers of the government been ordered to forward materials to it, and its actual inauguration had been further delayed by over a decade. The speaker blamed no one for the holdup, applauding the good intentions of all. Speaking modestly, he asserted that a permanent record of Guatemala's past must be established as "a social necessity," even when the Indian past was so distant that it seemed of "natural" rather than human construction.

This museum would help Guatemala achieve cultural balance even as it sought economic growth based on agriculture. "Nascent arts and industry" must not be neglected just because agriculture was the obvious card Guatemala had to play on the world market. Machado finished his dedication with a classic argument from the humanities: Sentiment, reason, and action were the God-given faculties that produced the necessary activities of art, sciences, and industry. The Society's museum responded to another great objective, helping the nation delineate its own past. The citizen could see the civilization of earlier times and assess the progress attained in the sciences and arts. "The history of primitive America is important. . . . A Latin poet suggested 'I am man: to nothing of man can I be indifferent.' Thus we must learn the forgotten story of the indigenous races. We may be poor in art, but we are rich in nature."[44] Machado was indicating that foreigners would judge Guatemala's progress by museums of this sort, and another speaker underlined the nation's need for the kind of respectability that such a museum would provide. In the past distinguished foreign visitors had derided in print Guatemala's empty claim to such institutions.[45]

It was apparent at the end of 1865 that Guatemala had profited economically from the long period of peace and order imposed by Carrera's regime. The election of Cerna was meant to continue that regime indefinitely. Though not all realized it, Guatemala was face to face with the dilemma of all oligarchic Latin America: How would the social and economic institutions that guaranteed the position of the elite — that is, "order" in the social sense — be maintained at the same time progress and its profits were sought? Maximilian's ephemeral empire in Mexico excited the more conservative elements in and around the government, particularly ecclesiastical ones, but it soon passed away. Its passing revealed an age moving inexorably from monarchy toward republicanism and the continual development of socially disturbing technology. Still, the shadow of Carrera and the hand of the Church would hold the government of Guatemala in a firm grip through the 1860s.

Notes

1. Pedro Tobar Cruz, *Los montañeses*, 2nd ed. (Guatemala: Editorial del Ministerio de Educación Pública, 1959), passim; Ralph Lee Woodward, Jr., *Central America: A Nation Divided*, 2nd ed. (New York: Oxford University Press, 1985), 98–105.

2. John L. Stephens, *Incidents of Travel in Central America, Chiapas, and Yucatán*, vol. 2 (New York: Dover Publications, 1841), 60–61.

3. Woodward, *Central America*, 105; Clemente Marroquín Rojas, *Francisco Morazán y Rafael Carrera* (Guatemala: Imprenta Marroquín Hermanos, 1965), 118.

4. *Ibid.*, 143–146.

5. *Ibid.*, 160; for discussion of cruelty, see Tobar Cruz, *Los montañeses*, 118, 147–148.

6. Italo López Vallecillos, *Gerardo Barrios y su tiempo*, vol. 1 (San Salvador: Ministerio de Educación, 1967), 22–24.

7. Marroquín Rojas, *Morazán y Carrera*, 397–398.

8. See the dispatches of James Partridge (U.S. minister to Honduras): No. 24, San Salvador, February 12, 1863, on interview with Carrera; No. 25, San Salvador, February 25, 1863, notice of Carrera's defeat; No. 26, San Salvador, March 12, 1863, details of the battle; all in U.S. Archives Microfilms Publications, Film Microcopy 219, Roll 22 (hereinafter cited as FM 219, R 22).

9. Partridge (now minister to El Salvador), No. 5, San Salvador, July 26, 1863, pictures final destruction of the Gerardo Barrios regime; FM 219, R 23.

10. Partridge, San Salvador dispatches of August 1, August 23, August 30, September 1, September 27, October 1, October 12, 1863; and from La Unión,: October 15, November 4, 1863; FM 219, R 23.

11. Rafael Carrera, "A los gefes y soldados, San Salvador, Octubre 30, 1863," in *Gaceta de Guatemala* (hereinafter cited as *Gaceta*) XIV, 7 (November 16, 1863), 1.

12. Programa, *Gaceta* XIV, 8 (November 25, 1863), 1: and "El Salvador" (from *El Constitucional*, San Salvador, December 11, 1863), in *Gaceta* XIV, 10 (December 19, 1863), 6.

13. *Gaceta* XIV, 11 (December 31, 1863), 1.

14. Rafael Carrera, Mensaje, *Gaceta* XIV, 10 (December 19, 1863), 1.

15. *El mercurio*, Lima (February 27, 1864), in *Gaceta* XIV, 22 (April 19, 1864).

16. *Gaceta* XIV, 20 (March 21, 1864), 2–3; 22 (April 9, 1864), 2; 35 (July 16, 1864),1–2; 23 (April 18, 1864), 3; 42 (September 14, 1864), 1; 49 (November 11, 1864), 1; 51 (November 29, 1864), 5; and 52 (December 3, 1864), 2.

17. *Gaceta* XIV, 48 (November 3, 1864), 1–2.

18. Rafael Carrera, Mensaje, November 25, 1864, *Gaceta* XIV, 51 (November 29, 1864), 1–3.

19. "Algunas observaciones respecto a la última guerra," *Gaceta* XIV, 53 (December 11, 1864), 2.

20. *La revista* (New York), commented on and quoted in "Nóvo periódicos," *Gaceta* XIV, 53 (December 11, 1864), 2.

21. "Respeto a la voluntad nacional," *Gaceta* XIV, 54 (December 11, 1864), 2.

22. José Telésforo Paúl, S.J., *Oración fúnebre del Excelentísimo Sr. Capitán General Don Rafael Carrera* (Guatemala, April 1865), Latin American Library, Tulane University.

23. *Ibid.*, 19, 22, 37; *Gaceta* XIV, 78 (July 12, 1865). The theocratic dictator of Ecuador, Gabriel García Moreno, had issued the joint eulogy in a decree of mourning.

24. "Crédito público," *Gaceta* XIV, 72 (May 8, 1865), 5, notes private loans to the government to aid transition; "Elección de presidente de la república," same page, reviews Cerna's qualifications. Also, dispatch of Charles N. Riotte (U.S. minister to Costa Rica), No. 137, San José, December 10, 1865, renders a favorable, if lukewarm, judgment on Cerna.

25. The best general reference work on Napoleon III's career is William E. Echard, ed., *Historical Dictionary of the French Second Empire, 1852–1870* (Westport, CT: Greenwood Press, 1985); see also Stuart L. Campbell, *The Second Empire Revisited, a Historiography* (New Brunswick, NJ: Rutgers University Press, 1978).

26. Alfred J. and Kathryn A. Hanna, *Napoleon III and Mexico: American Triumph over Monarchy* (Chapel Hill: University of North Carolina Press, 1971), 67.

27. *Ibid.* More difficult to obtain but probably the most sophisticated analysis of Napoleon III's Mexican venture is John L. Phelan, "Pan-Latinism, French Intervention in Mexico (1861–1867) and the Genesis of the Idea of Latin America," in Juan A. Ortega y Medina, ed., *Conciencia y autenticidad históricas. México. Escritos en homenaje a Edmundo OGorman* (Mexico: UNAM, 1968), 279–298.

28. William E. Duvall, "Bonapartism," in Echard, *Historical Dictionary of the French Second Empire*, 60–62.

29. "Variedades," *Gaceta* XIV, 71 (April 28, 1865), 6–7.

30. E. G. Masseras, "Méjico, el programa del imperio," parts I–IV, *Gaceta* XIV, 38 (August 9, 1864), 2–4, and parts V–VIII, 39 (August 16, 1864), 3–5.

31. Echard, "Corps legislatif," *Historical Dictionary of the French Second Empire, 1852–1870*, 130–143.

32. Masseras, "Méjico," *Gaceta* XIV, 39 (August 16, 1864), 6.

33. *Gaceta* XV, 19 (June 25, 1866), 151–153; 25 (September 1, 1866); 45 (May 11, 1867); 48 (June 5, 1867), 383; 52 (July 19, 1867), 415; 57 (September 6, 1867), 455.

34. The essays by various authors in Joseph L. Love and Nils Jacobsen, eds., *Guiding the Invisible Hand; Economic Liberalism and the State in Latin American History* (New York: Praeger Publishers, 1988), provide the most sophisticated composite view of nineteenth-century Latin American economic ideology to date. For the isthmus, see Ralph Lee Woodward, Jr., "The Rise and Decline of Liberalism in Central America: Historical Perspectives on the Contemporary Crisis," *Journal of Inter-American Studies and World Affairs* 26 (August, 1984), 291–312.

35. José Milla, "Discurso en elogio de Fr. Matías Córdova ... 13 de enero de 1867," *Sociedad Económica* I, 9 (January 1867), 170.

36. "Elección de presidente de la república," *Gaceta* XIV, 72 (May 8, 1865), 5; and "Mensaje dirijido por el Sr. Ministro encargado ...," 72 (May 8, 1865), 1.

37. *Ibid.*, 5.

38. "Crédito público," *Gaceta* XIV, 72 (May 8, 1865), 5; Vicente Cerna, "Manifiesto del excmo, presidente de la nación, 24 de mayo de 1865," 74 (May 29, 1865), 1.

39. "Convite," *Gaceta* XIV, 74 (May 29, 1865), 4–5.

40. Ministerio de la guerra, *Gaceta* XIV, 77 (July 4, 1865), 2; "Emigrados políticos," 77 (July 4, 1865), 4.

41. *Ibid.*

42. "Aniversario de independencia," *Gaceta* XIV, 88 (September 15, 1865), 6–7. Cf. Jorge Skinner-Klee, *Revolución y derecho: una investigación sobre el problema de la revolución en el derecho guatemalteco* (Guatemala: Ministerio de Educación, 1971), 65–74, for a careful application of Crane Brinton's ideas of revolution to this period.

43. "Situación de la república," *Gaceta* XIV, 92 (October 17, 1865), 1.

44. Rafael Machado, Discurso, *Sociedad económica* I, 1 (January 1866), 5–8.

45. J. R. Rodríguez, "Memoria ... 28 diciembre de 1865," *Sociedad económica* I, 1 (January 1866), 9–10.

2
Consensus, 1865–1869

During the three or four decades after independence, many Spanish Americans looked for a non-Hispanic political formula to solve their problems and build toward the future. Europe provided a treasury of political thought, and the United States, known to its admirers in Latin America as "the great republic," also furnished compelling models. These appeared often in Spanish American constitutions, but, as in the case of the Central American Federation, they usually failed to solve the problems at hand. After numerous failures of such exotic political experiments, elites in the region turned increasingly to economic solutions as a first concern. Many came to believe that a political solution would derive naturally from a stable society and successful economy, rather than the reverse. Thus, foreign theories that professed to be materially systemic (such as Darwinism) or historically systemic (such as Comtean positivism) became widely attractive in the region after 1860.

Foreign technologies also influenced events in Central America. The completion of the Panama railroad in 1855 accelerated economic development in the region. Just as the California gold rush in 1849 gave enormous momentum to the westward expansion of the United States, so the Panama railroad spurred economic change in Central America. A remarkable transfer of isthmian economic activity from the Caribbean to the Pacific followed. Pacific ports offered easier access to interior markets than did Caribbean ones; although most rivers drained into the Caribbean, they did not serve as major transportation conduits for most of Central America.[1]

Important as it was, the Panama railroad provided only an interim resolution of the larger isthmian transit question. One could argue that the whole character of Central American history was determined by that question — from the maneuvers of Francisco Pizarro in the sixteenth century to those of Omar Torrijos in the twentieth. Eventually, the issue boiled down to one project: a canal. Certainly the politics of canal-site selection were constant in the nineteenth century before and after construction of the railroad. A canal was important to the British and their Central American agent, Frederick Chatfield. It was important to the United States from the time of the acquisition of California, as demonstrated by negotiation of the Clayton-Bulwer Treaty of 1850 and construction of the Panama railroad. Napoleon III tied most of his Central American interests to that question. The so-called National War (1855–1857), in which Central American governments joined briefly to expel North American filibusters led by William Walker, was an immediate consequence of the quickening canal issue.

Several kinds of new technology entered Central America during the next twenty years. Unlike some Spanish American nations, Guatemala, under the firm hand of General Carrera, experienced relative peace after 1840 and especially after 1851. This stability prepared it to receive more technology, to experience a degree of modernization, and (in the vocabulary of the day), to progress. The technology of coffee culture was introduced early on, about the time the Panama railroad was completed. Coffee developed rapidly, but otherwise Guatemala had not progressed far by 1863.

Guatemala's Worldview in the 1860s

In that turbulent year, which saw Carrera's triumphant siege of San Salvador, an impressive essay was undertaken to depict the current state of Guatemala. It was written by Enrique Palacios, a well-educated, polished young Guatemalan who had won Carrera's approval and was then serving as minister to Nicaragua. Apparently he wrote the essay to pass the time while on diplomatic assignment, thinking it was needed to attract immigration. Palacios completed the essay in Nicaragua late in 1864 and sent it to the newest, most prestigious journal in Guatemala City, La semana, just after its inauguration in January 1865. The essay, Reseña de la situación general de Guatemala, 1863, was published under the pseudonym Pio Casals in sixteen installments between April and July 1865, precisely bridging Carrera's illness and death and the conversion to the Cerna regime. Noting the lack of attention given Guatemala by the outside world, Palacios distinguished it from some other Spanish American nations:

"In effect," he wrote, "Guatemala is one of the few republics that has wisely profited from an unfortunate era common to all the former Spanish colonies by establishing a regime based not on prestigious theories but upon its adequacy to meet the country's social condition. Thus Guatemala has obtained peace for a quarter of a century using only its own modest forces to march firmly on the road of progress." And yet, suggested Palacios, there had been no adequate report on these admirable achievements. A handful of archaeologists had visited Guatemala in search of Mayan ruins, and other observant visitors had "crafted tales and pretensions of history," but they did not really describe the vigor and abundance that Palacios saw. What was needed was a description of "this very privileged region" that would cause Europeans to move to Guatemala and do their civilizing work in it.[2]

Palacios spoke for the oligarchy, a notably literary group,[3] assembling available social and economic data to show what the country's longtime conservative regime had accomplished. He maintained, as did all knowledgeable witnesses, that Guatemala's wealth and potential were primarily agricultural. Excluding cochineal (a material used in dye), Guatemala's annual production of agricultural wealth was eighteen times greater in 1862 than in 1852 (18,950 pesos in 1852, 247,290 in 1862), Palacios asserted. Though a check of his calculation indicates that the 1862 production figure was only thirteen times greater, it still illustrates the impressive development of agriculture under the Carrera regime. The figures on cochineal were kept separately because they were huge for those years, dwarfing the figures for all other commodities combined. But cochineal crop production and the world market for it were both unstable, and its future value to the national economy appeared to be precarious. Palacios argued that although the Carrera regime's economy had been built upon exports of cochineal, its decreasing reliability had caused the state to encourage development of coffee as a replacement. He concluded that the new export crop bid fair to dominate the next generation much as cochineal had the last.

The tone of this essay and of the Guatemalan press in general was that of an oligarchy talking to itself and some of its retainers. When leaders wished to talk to a wider audience, selections from *La semana* and the *Gaceta* were reprinted as pamphlets or broadsides. Thus, editorial discussion in *La semana* of the death of General Carrera buttressed the memory of the captain general and president-for-life as a man of Providence. This coverage rebutted charges from Central American liberals such as Gerardo Barrios that Carrera was merely the puppet of a narrow conservative cabal. With almost Pythagorean imagery, *La semana* noted that he had first entered

Guatemala City with his peasant army on April 13, 1839, and had died there, ending his rule only with his life, on April 14, 1865, twenty-six years and a day later. "How little signify human calculations before these mysterious figures. It is necessary to see providential designs in this, since it is not possible to explain it with that empty, illogical, absurd word called chance. We shall try to show ... that what can be done has been done in order that General Carrera's accomplishment will survive, and that in all probability it will not end with his life, as some are prophesying."[4]

Imputation of divine significance to Carrera was combined with careful approval of the first presidential message from his successor, Gen. Vicente Cerna, who expressed "elevated political thought which satisfied the desires of every good citizen who loves the glory and legitimate progress of his country." Echoing Palacios, the editor noted that the exaggerated principles and faddish theories that had fed public sentiment in other times could not achieve great objectives. He emphasized that the calm of Cerna's message, characterized by "modest words, without boasting of threats or force," was appropriate.[5]

The political nemesis of Cerna's succession appeared in the form of Gerardo Barrios. This former president of El Salvador, defeated and forced into exile by Carrera, remained the most articulate liberal in Central America, and he continued to alarm the elite in Guatemala City. After a brief trip to the United States, he based his political and military activities in Costa Rica. In the standard unionist manner, Barrios viewed Central America as a single arena. With allies from Honduras and Nicaragua, he tried to retake El Salvador. Failing in his attempt, he fled south on a sailing ship, only to be captured in Nicaraguan waters by local authorities in apparent collaboration with Enrique Palacios, still Guatemalan minister to Nicaragua.

This action and its results read like Greek tragedy. Palacios received a near-fatal gunshot wound from an assassin, apparently in retaliation for his violation of comity regarding political exiles. The Nicaraguan government, previously hesitant to respond to El Salvador's request for Barrios's extradition, finally did so in the emotional aftermath of the attack on Palacios. El Salvador's government promised Nicaragua it would not impose the death penalty if extradition were granted but later reversed itself under pressure from Guatemala. Barrios was executed by firing squad.[6] Removal of this liberal spinner of "glittering theories" relieved conservatives in Guatemala City, who sought in El Salvador quiet acceptance of an orderly regime directed by the best people.

Self-congratulation at Cerna's smooth succession now infused commentary in *La semana*, which noted that the presidential-selection mechanism established in the Acta Constituva of 1851 had been used for the first
time and had worked perfectly. The process amounted to indirect election
by secret ballot of the legislature; as it was described, the representatives of
the people and the great corporations named the "first magistrate of the
Republic." It was claimed that the world at large conceded this to be the
best system — to have the best persons choose the head of government in
the name of the people.[7] In earlier years it sometimes had been difficult to
get the best persons to serve in the assembly. In the current situation, that
was not the case: "Today it can be said that there are gathered in the
Chamber almost all the most notable persons in the Republic, [judged] by
their intelligence, propriety, political antecedents, and social position. In
this the Chamber is the true expression of the country; the different social
classes being represented in it." This was seen as a real achievement,
particularly in an age when unprincipled tactics in elections of deputies
were well known, even in countries with the most widely spread education
and most advanced constitutional government.

In Guatemala, political debates were limited to a small circle without
benefit of organized parties, but "there is never heat and disturbance in the
elections, nor do intrigues and subornation come into play." Some had
charged that power determined Guatemalan elections, but *La semana's*
writer did not see much to be gained by allowing the intrigue of a few corrupt
party leaders to replace the influence of established authority. Everywhere
it existed, the parliamentary system revealed serious inconveniences.
Where lay the advantage? "If it is bad that a Prefect or a Corregidor may
furnish the voting lists, it does not seem better to us that votes may be
bought publicly and that nominations are proposed in meetings where the
electors are saturated with whiskey or beer. In both cases it may be alleged
that deputies so elected are not the true and legitimate expression of
opinion and of public necessities." Compromise seemed to be indicated in
Guatemala, in *La semana's* view; taking into account its diverse population
and the low literacy of its masses, the country should content itself with a
representative body of decent and respectable persons of good will, individuals well versed in public affairs. "More than that is to ask the impossible
for now, and would expose us to the fall into anarchy and dislocation to
which unfortunately many hispanic-American republics are seen reduced,
with all their liberal theories, understood as they may be in those countries."[8]

La semana persisted in its strong, almost obsessive judgment that Guatemala under Carrera had stolen a march on much of Spanish America by eschewing liberal theory, experiencing instead a long, constructive period of peace. At the end of *La semana*'s first year of publication, its editor expressed a desire for "true progress" so that his country could follow peaceful pursuits without distracting tensions. He saw the peaceful succession of Cerna as evidence of the new leader's worthiness and of the solidity of Guatemala's institutions. Indeed, he theorized that *La semana* itself was "truly liberal" because it avoided exaggeration and demagogy![9]

The need for concentrated authority in a developing country soon prompted a critique of laissez-faire policy, another aspect of nineteenth-century liberalism. The editor argued cogently that large, well-developed countries can wait for the initiative of private enterprise because they have so much of it. Small, developing countries, however, could not afford to wait: state authority should become more active, since little was to be hoped for from private enterprise. Subsidies to new branches of agriculture, exclusive — that is, monopolistic — privileges for introduction of new industries, and other measures to encourage development of public wealth were good. Authority was thought to include not only government but "all those in the capital city and in the departmental centers who have the administration of public affairs in their care." The government by itself could do little without efficacious support, but if it called "the men most honored, intelligent and patriotic" to public posts, these would in turn cooperate in the country's work of progress, "favoring individual enterprise and . . . projects not initiated by this unfortunately quite limited [group]."[10]

The comfortable, aristocratic, organic view of society expressed in *La semana* for the Guatemalan elite was, of course, related from time to time to international affairs. During the era of domestic good feelings in 1865–1866, the perplexing uncertainties presented by Maximilian's empire in Mexico still dominated foreign policy considerations, but a calm view was taken of Central American affairs after elimination of Gerardo Barrios, and close relations were maintained with the Dueñas regime in El Salvador.[11] Historical and geographic ties with the rest of Central America were seen as fundamental despite the separatist stance Guatemala had adopted so successfully under Carrera: "The community of origin, religion, language, customs, etc., tie us to the other Sections of Central America in a manner more immediate than to any other on the American Continent. That community, we say, which causes the foreigner to look at these five States as if they were a single nationality, obliges us to give frequent attention to events in the other four Republics." It had been demonstrated that politics in any one of these countries could affect the others profoundly — thus the obvious need for these states to keep an eye on each other. The fact that events in El Salvador and Honduras were discussed more than those in Nicaragua and Costa Rica derived from the mere circumstance that mail came weekly from the first two but only twice a month from the more distant neighbors.[12]

Mundane discussion turned to opportunistic polemic whenever international events alarmed the editor or suggested a political lesson. The notorious Morant Bay uprising in Jamaica in late 1865 — put down with such brutal effectiveness that it became part of the language of reform politics in Victorian England — brought acid comment in Guatemala City. News arrived in the Belize mail packet in January 1866 of the complaints by British reformers ("los amigos de los negros") about the cruelty with which Jamaica was pacified and their demands for an investigating committee. Wrote *La semana*, "It seems that those gentlemen who are such friends of the blacks profess the system of 'kill the society in order to save the principles.' The liberalism of English institutions, by whose kindness the emancipated slaves of Jamaica were made participants, has resulted, sadly, lamentably, in an inundation of bloodshed on the island." Simply put, the editor blamed the massacre on a lapse of authority over incompetent freedmen. To Guatemalan conservatives, Morant Bay signified no more than the foolishness of liberal theories.[13]

Looking further afield, those same conservatives took a philosophic view of the 1866 Spanish "naval war" on the Pacific coast of South America and seemed to deprecate "these nascent states" of Latin America. It called for calm observance of international treaties, saying the South American republics involved — Ecuador, Peru, and Chile — should make offensive-defensive alliances and call out the rest of Spanish America (as they had done) only if their independence were threatened. But no such threat existed here — there was just a terrible misunderstanding between the Hispanic nations involved. The entire discussion seemed apologetic to Europe, certainly not sympathetic to the Pacific coast states whose ports had been shelled by a Spanish naval squadron.[14]

This apparent put-down of South American states was reinforced in January 1867 by events in Guatemala. Field Marshal Serapio Cruz revolted, disturbing the regime and threatening Guatemala with a cycle of caudillismo such as other Spanish American states suffered. Guatemala seemed in danger of slipping off its ledge of order into anarchy, sharpening conservatives' distaste for the Latin American condition. The Hispanic republics again became the horrible example that must not be followed. Guatemala gained most when men of quality dedicated themselves to study of the practical questions of developing wealth, not to discussion of abstract political principles hardly applicable to a heterogeneous society. For an educated class — an insignificant minority — to engage in the latter activity when it had observed those principles create chaos in society was to court irresponsibility.

> We do not believe it is suitable to judge the country by the few educated men enclosed in the capital and some departmental centers: the great mass of the nation should be kept in view and its tendencies studied to understand its true needs and problems. Peace, justice, instruction, tranquillity, remunerated work, protection, are what claim preference for the immense majority of the population, composed of diverse races, some of which are today, by force of circumstance, in almost the same situation as they have been for 300 years. It would be an unfortunate error to judge the spirit of the majority of the nation, that which it needs and agrees to, by the spirit, needs and exigencies of several hundred educated men, a drop lost in a vast ocean.

The editor wished fervently that Guatemala were among the most advanced nations in the world with a culturally integrated citizenry but felt obliged to recognize that it was not. He held further that Spanish American nations generally did not provide a model for such attainments. Rather, they showed the way to "disquiet, backwardness, discredit, anarchy and ruin."[15]

Peace Advocacy

In 1867 news from Spanish America arrived at San José on the Panama steamer every two weeks, and it spoke of both internal and international wars. Quite aside from Mexico, indecipherable in the last months of Maximilian's rule, the republics to the south seemed a labyrinth of revolutions. Personal interests paraded as public interest, and "the most sacred rights of man are infringed and the sources of moral and material advance are blocked" in the name of liberty and progress. "How else can one interpret what we see in . . . Colombia, in Ecuador, in Venezuela, in Peru and in the . . . Plata?" asked *La semana*. "What are the saving principles, what is the positive good established and supplied by those disturbances that decimate population, create inextinguishable hatreds, destroy credit, and keep industry, agriculture, mining and commerce in lamentable backwardness?"

Latin American republics needed public education, roads, immigration, and other "positive" improvements. Could these be attained if citizens scarcely had time to defend their lives and property and were constantly exposed to a senseless, terrible game of revolutions? "The press of those countries covers crimes and disasters every day, and in the midst of that chaos of anarchy and ruins we do not see what humanity gains, how civilization advances," *La semana* charged. Instead, barbarism gained ground in the presence of great natural resources in Peru and Colombia; peoples who ought to be astonishingly prosperous were not. Yet, observed the editorial, some believed that such destruction would regenerate societies! Further, the people of Guatemala, who enjoyed tranquility, security, and avoidance of South America's "horrendous spectacles," paradoxically were told by critics — such as exiled liberals — that they enjoyed the peace of the tomb! To men who valued "their repose, wellbeing, families and fortune, the events occurring in the hispanic-American Republics" should provide a grim warning; people who loved disorder were reminded that "those who promote anarchy are regularly its first victims." Peaceful, moderate citizens are not after perfection and the dangers of the unknown; they appreciate what they have now as opposed to the uncertain path of upheavals. Such persons, *La semana* urged, ought to consider what is happening in strife-filled countries and "with hand on heart say whether they want a similar situation for their country."[16]

This castigation of other Spanish American countries, at the very time Maximilian's effort to establish pan-Latinism was failing, set political guidelines that the Cerna regime pursued to the end: (1) Peace was a benefit in itself; (2) Guatemala should not imitate foreign political models because doing so would distract from the priority work of developing the country materially; and (3) although government initiative was needed, progress required unity and a fair effort by all.[17]

This notion of peace was deployed through several devices. On the one hand, President Cerna toured the departments preaching civil tranquility as the prime necessity for progress.[18] On the other, an editor explaining the difficulties of putting out an interesting journal held that in a peaceful situation no news literally was good news and quoted the French proverb — *point de nouvelle, bonnes nouvelle* — to that effect. He proceeded to the homily that false news, which was a temptation in this situation, was like a rumor — it always required both an inventor and the gullible. He duly noted the moral defects of both.

"The lack of news makes very difficult the discharge of duties imposed by journalism," he asserted. "To fill a journal with [foreign] reproductions is a very easy task, but does not satisfy those who wish to be informed of the news which occurs in the country." Organs of public information had become so numerous by the 1860s, especially in Europe and America, that all events were treated more or less profoundly in them. The problem of Guatemalan journalism remained. "It has been said many times that the work of journalism is more difficult and slippery among us than in other places. Without a great political, economic and intellectual movement, the press is normally obliged to carry on a precarious existence, and to live by borrowing, copying that which is written elsewhere." Readers would have to adjust and indulge writers who could not find material for an article in depth.[19]

This problem of boredom in the early Cerna regime called forth other analogies, including biological ones. "Public tranquility is for societies what health is for the body!" wrote *La semana*, triumphantly reporting that June 1866 had passed without a disturbance in any of the isthmian countries. "Thus, as in the midst of anarchy, the former is craved and appreciated; so also when physical pains overwhelm the patient who is their prisoner the value of health is better recognized." The government and the public each needed to work for peace in order to maintain progress, but "it is the government's responsibility to give the social machine the necessary impulse."[20]

Both the concept of peace as *magnum bonum*, elaborated after the Cruz revolt of 1867, and the idea of the inevitability of gradual change, always present in the Cerna regime, were promoted with strong Burkean undertones. This held true for the regime's view of Central America and of Spanish America generally. A series of articles on "The Conservative Spirit and Reform" in autumn 1867 viewed the course of recent Central American history as almost inevitable. The borrowing of political theory from the French Revolution of 1789, the Spanish Constitution of 1812, and the United States resulted in an understandable but "strange" amalgam by 1829. This new order was so alien to the masses, accustomed to the institutions and social habits of the Spanish empire, that a slow ferment of discontent had resulted, overlooked by the reformist rulers. The time bomb eventually was detonated by the "absurd idea" that the government had poisoned the waters, causing the cholera epidemic of 1837. The mass revolt led by Carrera followed.

"The order of things inaugurated in 1839 had to be reactionary," *La semana* declared. "The revolution proclaimed the restoration of the old, but this new order was vigorous and energetic because it derived its force from the opinion of the great majority of the country." Between 1821 and 1838, different groups in the elite had dominated, seeking ideal democracy, and the resulting excesses of demagogy had inevitably paved the way to military dictatorship. In placing blame for that development, it seemed more judicious to attribute it to the times or to a lack of appropriate social experience than to individuals. Yet it was duly noted that some individuals who were known to have provoked the popular revolt of 1837–1838 through their "insensate determination to destroy necessary social elements" were the same ones who now anathematized that revolution and its results in the name of the people. Such behavior, such a political non sequitur, was common in human experience, albeit astonishing. Still, *La semana* preferred to be clear on such matters.

> We have said it already: we are not opposed to reforms and we are very far from embracing the sad and disconsolate idea that societies have to remain stationary. Our aim has been . . . to make clear . . . that it is not convenient to attack the fundamental principles that serve as the base of our society, and that those principles are not incompatible with political, moral, intellectual and material progress. It can be improved in all areas without imprudently touching the constitutive elements of our nationality, leaving to time and to the advance of civilization the care of reforming that which is essentially vicious or incompatible with the spirit of the century.[21]

The editor asserted that cycles of radical reform and reaction such as had characterized Guatemala from 1829 to 1839 had occurred in a number of Spanish American states yet were notably absent from one of them: "Chile did not precipitously demolish its ancient social organization. Very little was changed after proclaiming its independence, and even today there continue in that Republic many antique institutions which reformers have declared irreconcilable with all progress and civilization." Yet civilization and progress had developed in Chile "beside those ancient vestiges of another time" with astonishing and enviable speed. Improvements in education, agriculture, commerce, and industry had not been blocked by traditional institutions. On the contrary, it appeared that if Chile had indulged in radical reform after the 1820s, it might find itself in the kind of mess in the 1860s that existed in Mexico, with all its reforms. Such reforms retarded progress instead of speeding it because they introduced confusion, provoked resistance, and incited civil war, destroyer of progress in those countries.

The benefits of moderation simply had to be considered. Since the existing structure of Guatemalan society consisted of either "remains from the colonial domination" or new elements created since 1839 — the intervening reform period of the federation having been filled with sterile projects — the status quo should be treated gently. Improvements in public administration could be made through the old institutions. "To declare war on the religion of the immense majority of the inhabitants; to assault property; to condemn unreflectingly the ancient laws and customs equates, we repeat, with blocking all true progress in countries constituted like ours." Competence was demonstrated by improvements that did not destroy the basis of society, the combination of conservative elements with progress and ideas of civilization. This possibility was shown by the examples of Chile and of Guatemala:

> We repeat that for us there are no absolute principles in politics, other than the eternal notions of justice that have universal application. Thus it may very well happen that time will alter profoundly the structure of these societies; that European immigration may modify them substantially and may come to make of them something similar to what exists in the United States, for example. Then will be the time for reforming that which today is indispensably necessary but which will come to be useless and a stumbling block. But while our political realities are what they are today, and give evidence of continuing to be so for a long time, civilization, progress and true liberty can only exist by preserving their constituent elements.[22]

Later, when the Cerna regime entered its final period of crisis in the spring of 1869, it would reiterate this general argument, changing only the details.[23]

Good Works

A conservative ideology professing the value of pragmatism could remain credible only by pragmatic accomplishments. The physical and technological infrastructure of Guatemala City and of the country provided an obvious gauge by which to measure these efforts. The regime touted its achievements in at least four areas: internal transportation, port facilities, domestic commerce, and communication. One can in turn reduce these development programs under Cerna to two categories: modernization of

transportation and communication on the one hand and rational improvement of domestic commerce and order on the other.

The agency in charge of improving transportation during most of the
century was the Consulado de Comercio in Guatemala City, a monopolistic
merchant guild chartered by the government of Spain in 1793. It had
survived independence until the liberals suppressed it in 1829. Revived ten
years later by the Carrera revolution, the consulado had shared governance
since. The government delegated to it formal authority for maintenance,
planning, and development of the nation's road system. The word "formal"
must be emphasized: Though ample funds were dedicated to the consulado
for these purposes, through the decades the government often, almost
habitually, borrowed those funds for other purposes. Thus, the consulado
never had the capital necessary for an adequate transportation system. Also,
it is certain that President Carrera pressured the consulado into supporting
his favorite projects. Of these, the Zacapa–Guatemala City carriage road
in the 1850s was best known.[24]

During Carrera's last illness, a new wave of speculation about road
systems appeared in the Guatemala City press. The decline of the Belize
trade in the decade after the Panama railroad opened remained a concern.
A number of new approaches to transportation were suggested as the Cerna
regime got under way, and a significantly new system of roads was proposed
by 1866. The Verapaz region had great potential for new coffee cultivation
if provided a means of transport. By 1866, a veteran government engineer
who specialized in roads, Salvador Cobos, had completed the survey for a
carretera formal from Tactic to Telemán on the river Polochic, a distance
of thirteen leagues (about thirty-nine miles). The project was considered
too expensive but so important to the developing coffee industry that it
must at least be started.[25] Also in the wind was the possibility of a better
road or even a railroad to San Salvador. Population density along this route
made it seem likely to pay off in ordinary commercial terms.

One official thought such a variety of projects constituted integral
development.[26] However, Cobos and his associate Vicente Zebadua warned
that such enthusiasm risked outstripping the means available to government and consulado in the immediate future. The consulado had been
urged to undertake a number of projects, but the specialists presented a plan
based only upon the agency's past and projected revenues — and thus, they
implied, upon reality. They asserted that their plan would bring good
practical results in improving roads for which funds had been earmarked:
"It is more convenient to our peculiar circumstances to go on improving
what we have with the elements at our disposal than to dream up projects

now unrealizable." Though many useful works had been projected, the great amount of time spent trying to get them started had resulted in nothing. Thus, "a general plan easy of execution which conforms to our capacities is without doubt more convenient." The run-down road system could be upgraded and made effective if the consulado concentrated its present means upon it.[27] Cobos and Zebadua confidently included a budget for their plan, but it was answered in the *Gaceta* by a critique favoring a new road system.[28]

After Cerna's government put down the Cruz revolt in 1867, the consulado's ambitions to modernize the transportation system appear to have become more urgent. Government rhetoric at that time indicated increased concern about loyalty of the country's elite, and the desire to attract coffee profits was clearly motivated by this concern. However, a modern upland plantation economy would require a much improved transportation network of roads and railroads for national distribution and exports. Little had been accomplished over the preceding decade, but now something changed. By 1868 a brother of the regime's sharpest parliamentary critic received a government contract to construct the first segment of railroad from San José to Escuintla. In the following year, as internal political debate heated up, the government became even more enthusiastic about projects uniting development and transportation improvement. An editorial in the *Gaceta*, captured this spirit: "The idea that individual well-being is intimately tied to the general progress of the nation can never be emphasized enough. In countries like ours, whose future depends principally upon exploitation of agriculture, projects which tend to fulfill that important objective ought to be received with the interest and sympathy that excites desire for the general advance."[29]

The editorialist believed the time had come for all to contribute to national prosperity, and he urged that a project of Father José Guell y Busquets to open lands for cultivation in the northern part of the country deserved full consideration. The initiative would offer lands adaptable to all types of plantings, lands containing beautiful forests comprising "a multitude of woods for dyes and construction. To place that means of advancement within the reach of many persons, the price of lots has been fixed at one hundred pesos, paid in installments collected three times a year." It was presented as a patriotic opportunity to prosper: "The exuberance of those lands, their situation near the Atlantic coast and Lake Izabal, the circumstance finally of being irrigated by the rich rivers which offer easy export to their products, merit the close attention of cultivators."

Father Busquets publicized the project extensively amid high hopes that Guatemalans would be interested. But if they were not, "Father Busquets is resolved to go to the island of Cuba in order to stimulate capitalists of that island to join the enterprise. We would hope that did not happen, although the prospect of attracting workers and resources from the exterior is certainly an attractive one." Plans for expeditious development of the project's communications and infrastructure were also announced in detail.[30] Objectively and symbolically, this project illustrated how the Cerna regime tried to foment progress, utilizing church personnel for secular leadership and control and soliciting the private sector for the necessary capital, all the while toying with the idea of going abroad for investors.

At that moment, Enrique Palacios, special envoy in the United States and Europe, made even more ambitious efforts to borrow £500,000 for Guatemala's internal improvements. Legislative authorization to seek a loan had been obtained as early as 1863, but negotiations had been delayed by European disturbances and the health of the Guatemalan minister to London and Paris. In 1868 Palacios, now considered a fiscal expert, was sent first to the United States, where he was unsuccessful, and then to Europe, where, with the advice of the veteran minister, he contracted a loan through the British house of Thompson, Bonar & Company. The government announced the loan's principal purpose to be improvement of the country's transportation system. "People are stimulated by routes of communication through exchange of their products and reciprocal transmission of their ideas; the roads, we say, looked upon everywhere as a sign of national culture, are now going to be a very special object of attention of the government when it has the pecuniary resources." Government spokesmen vowed that such projects would provide employment as well as moral and material advance for Guatemala.[31]

By 1870, under great pressure to make good on its promises, the government announced ostentatious plans for a railroad from the capital to the north coast. It defended its project by referring to a modern writer who asserted that "the railroad is the civilizing element par excellence, it is the herald of progress of the peoples; and there is nothing that can bring the pursuit of welfare and order with more efficacy than the iron rails that reduce long distances to a question of minutes." The *Gaceta* noted that providing for "the happiness of future generations" was one of the government's most imperious duties: "Our readers will do us the justice of agreeing that Señor General Cerna and his counselors work without rest in order to leave to his successors solid proofs of his zeal for the general welfare, thus stimulating his successors . . . [and] omitting no means of justifying the confidence of his present supporters." The government also assured supporters that English engineers were busy surveying the route. Soon thereafter the *corregidor* of Izabal reported the beginning of work on a canal from Lagartos Sound to connect with the Polochic River, and the Economic Society's journal, *Sociedad Económica*, ran a series of articles on current recommendations for general repair of the existing road system.[32]

The rationale for railroads and a better road system to foster foreign trade applied equally well to the need for an effective port. Throughout the nineteenth century, Spanish and Republican governments had been pressed to establish such a facility.[33] In the 1850s and 1860s Guatemala sought it with increasing urgency, but a solution to the problem remained elusive. Until the late 1850s, Izabal, on the Caribbean north coast, had served as a port, but it had never been adequate: Roads on the long, difficult route from the capital deteriorated rapidly because of heavy rainfall. For significant stretches the route had remained only a mule trail.

Completion of the Panama railroad and establishment of effective steamer service along the Pacific coast of Central America brought matters to a head. The Pacific coast provided few sheltered harbors, none in Guatemala. The long search for a site finally settled on San José, and the port opened officially in 1853, but its wharf was not completed until 1857. Until then, cargoes were ferried to and from the beach from vessels anchored offshore. Construction of a wharf did not solve the problem because of the violent surf of an open coast and the heavy traffic that resulted from the trade shift to the Pacific. Thus, after 1858 the government sought construction of a much larger, heavier iron wharf.

In 1862 the government went further, contracting for a steel wharf at San José to be completed by the end of March 1864. However, the structure was not built, perhaps because of the 1863 war, and in 1866 a new contract was made with Guatemalan entrepreneur Pio Benito. The government was quick to explain that generous provisions in the contract, particularly the wharfage fees, derived from the national necessity. "The need . . . has grown more urgent with each passing day, as much to furnish useful and easy exit for our agricultural products, as for commerce to avoid damages and inflated costs," the *Gaceta* explained. "It has been necessary for the agreement to make ample concessions in order to get anyone to take over this costly and risky enterprise considering the natural difficulties which our coast presents for the erection and maintenance of such a wharf." The ample terms forbade any other wharf to be built within fifty miles of San José for fifty years; if the works were destroyed while under construction, the government would reimburse the entrepreneur half of the cost and guarantee him an income of 75,000 pesos for two years. Beyond that, the government guaranteed an income from the wharf of 25,000 pesos per annum for twenty years; moreover, government port employees and mail service would not be paid from wharf fees.[34]

The need for this extensive wharf remained obvious, as when, in September 1867, the steamer *Parkersburg* was delayed a day putting off the mails and taking on passengers because of dangerous crosscurrents. The completed wharf represented a solid accomplishment by the Cerna government; it opened the country to commercial intercourse in a way never before experienced. It seemed appropriate at the wharf's opening for public traffic on July 18, 1868, to have it "adorned with flags and banners in its entire extension with three boats anchored in the roadstead dressed in similar fashion."[35]

The administration also boasted of material progress by other conservative isthmian regimes. The Dueñas government's opening of a similar wharf in El Salvador at the port of Libertad in October 1869 was duly applauded in the *Gaceta*, as was the initially successful effort of conservative president José María Medina of Honduras to promote a transisthmian railroad in that country.[36]

Railroads, steamships, steel wharves, and new public buildings all were symbols of material progress to the Guatemalan elite. The first three in particular seemed the essence of modernization for them. The telegraph, which revolutionized communications from the middle of the nineteenth century, seemed no less so. The laying of trans-Atlantic submarine cables by the 1860s caused Latin America to quicken to possibilities of a brand-new informational relationship with the outside world. By the summer of 1867, the new possibilities were being reported in Guatemala City: "Through these [telegraph lines] the work of placing in instant communication the most extreme and remote points in the land will be seen as progress. It being possible to infer also that once the cables now being submerged in the Gulf of Mexico are established perhaps it will not be long before Central America, the link between two continents, can participate in the advantages of the incredible speed of communications that electricity furnishes." It was clear that if North America were connected with the southern continent, the wire would have to pass through Guatemala or its coastal waters. Thus, a newly chartered and organized telegraph company in Guatemala City soon became functional. In October 1867, the management announced arrival in Guatemala of materials needed for the telegraph, and at that time the funds previously pledged for shares in the company were called in.[37]

On May 3, 1868, the first telegraph messages in Guatemala were exchanged, covering six leagues (about eighteen miles) from the capital to Amatitlán. Not surprisingly, *La semana* made this event the lead story in its next issue, reporting it in detail. Organizers of the company had obtained a government monopoly for telegraph lines and had planned that the project's first stage should go only as far as Amatitlán. President Cerna urged the directors to extend lines to San José as quickly as possible, the utility of instant communication between the capital and the country's main port being obvious. In any case, telegraph service in the country had commenced, and the oligarchy had played its part smoothly: "Some young men trained by the Rev. Father Lizarzaburu of the Company of Jesus and by the engineer Don Salvador Cobos, transmit despatches regularly." The Baron Oscar Du Teil, principal director of the company and a member of the growing foreign commercial community, had provided the driving force behind the enterprise, and he received credit for bringing the telegraph to Guatemala several years earlier than would otherwise have been the case.

The president and ministers of government visited the telegraph office and exchanged dispatches with the corregidor of Amatitlán. Both messages commented that the telegraph was a luxury for Guatemala but signified progress for the country. The consensus was that time would convert the telegraph into an item of prime necessity now that the first difficult step had been taken. Two months later a public announcement indicated that the telegraph office was open and operating from Guatemala City to Amatitlán at the rate of two reales per twenty words, with an extra half-real charge for home delivery.[38] (A real equals about one-eighth of a peso.) It appears, however, that the system did not have much utility until the lines were extended further after 1871.

Such improvements in the national infrastructure, particularly in the capital, went forward steadily under Cerna, though not on a grand scale. Completion of one fundamental project in Guatemala City, a new public market to facilitate domestic commerce, required his entire term of office. Construction of the new building was distinctly a part of the movement for progress and modernization. The old market had become a scandal to modernizers and apparently to more traditional types as well. Land next to the cathedral, the Plazuela del Sagrario, was the preferred site, and appropriate arrangements were negotiated with the Church hierarchy.[39]

The principle organs of elite opinion explained and discussed the plans at length in mid-1866. Despite disagreement over the extent of land involved — *La semana* reported the dimensions as about 80 yards by 48, *Sociedad Económica* as 149 by 84 — there was early consensus on the need for and general location of the new market. The writer in *Sociedad Económica* argued for it on the bases of hygiene and aesthetics: "We shall see those ugly stalls which are called chests (*cajones*) replaced by clean and useful shops; those primitive tents (*parasoles*) which give such a savage aspect to our present market are going to disappear. It will be possible to classify and to inspect conveniently the diverse articles of nourishment and they will not be as now a confused and repugnant heap on the nasty pavement." It was noted that construction plans called for the use of native materials. "There is in this a sentiment of patriotic philanthropy, which will give work to a great number of our artisans and workers and will pour out among them the sum of 113,000 pesos which has been calculated as its cost." Pride in the project related it to the science of treatment of foods (*bramatología*), punctuated by the cliché "You are what you eat."[40]

Actual construction was delayed more than two years until the autumn of 1869 and followed revised plans drawn by a new architect. Commentary seemed to reflect the developing political crisis: "In conclusion, permit us to express to the corporation our desire that the building which is going to be constructed be named the Mercado Cerna. This desire signifies no more than a small testimony of our support for the present chief of the Republic."[41] Seven weeks later President Cerna himself laid the cornerstone in a full dress ceremony.

A year later it was noted that the soon-to-be-finished market would offer exciting new possibilities for feeding the people of the city, from an edifice worthy of a civilized community. The new market was expected to facilitate meat supply, which was poor in Guatemala City. It was noted that the Frenchman Edmund Carré had invented a portable refrigerator whose temperature could be kept at five degrees above zero for weeks on end. Thus, fish could be brought to Guatemala City from the ocean in light carriages. "Since we have ice available the entire year, the fish could be distributed easily in the new market. The day fresh fish is abundant in the market will be one of progress which few of us have thought about. Humble people's health will improve because they won't have to eat bad pork and [others] won't have to buy bad beef."[42]

Maintaining Order

In matters of public order, an elitist approach to the police problem illustrated the consensus within which Cerna's regime operated. Although visions of progress tended to ignore some ordinary social problems, the latter persisted and required practical solutions. Economic improvement in the 1860s does not appear to have brought a significant increase in criminal activity, but perhaps better times made the upper class less tolerant of malingering. In 1864 a general plan for expanding the jails was drawn up, and a reform of criminal law was given renewed consideration. By early 1866 the government had authorized the city council in the capital to proceed with this work. The rationale for an improved jail included, inevitably, commentary on the philosophy of corrections systems; authorities such as Bentham and Carnot were cited in passing, but serious discussion took on a distinctly local tone. By summer, construction was under way on the project known as "the reform of the jail building."[43]

Financing was arranged on a typically mixed base of public grants and private-sector loans. The cost was budgeted at 14,000 pesos, 10,000 of which came from the sale of 500-peso securities offered at moderate interest backed by dedication of a portion of the liquor tax. Government grants came in the form of 4,000 pesos raised from Supreme Court fines and 1,000 pesos from city council funds. At the end of July 1866, after construction had commenced, 3,000 pesos of the securities were still unsold, and the official press encouraged the elite to finish up this detail — noting that some patriots had bought securities and waived the interest. This friendly harangue was accompanied by serious discussion of the project, which was lauded as prudently planned. It was to include accommodations for jailers, shops, new cells (bartolinas), old cells, dormitories, separate quarters "for youths and decent persons," an infirmary pantry, and other offices.

A generous and broad-minded statement indicated how the new prison signified progress: "A building ample, commodious, healthy and secure has been arranged for the jail, in order to alleviate the sad situation of the unfortunates who society separates temporarily from its midst and deprives of liberty because of their offenses and faults." Religious sentiments were included: "The Christian thought and philosophy that has presided over the idea of that reform, is that of making the penalty for delinquents the least harsh possible and to establish appropriate separation among them, according to their condition and the nature of their crimes."[44]

No one could have thought, however, that the government was going soft. The murder of a prominent citizen in 1868 touched off demands for control of street crime and for reform of the police organization. Although performance of security officers and night police was considered satisfactory, "the daytime police are very far from being what they ought to be. Composed of the meager number of twenty gendarmes who go in groups of a half-dozen along regular routes far from areas where any disorder demands their presence, by no means do they effectively watch over a population of 40,000 inhabitants, circumscribed by a perimeter of about ten miles."

The kind of police department called for reveals something of the mind-set in the Guatemala City elite. The force was seen to be lacking the military unity and precision required to patrol the entire city, pursue delinquents, protect persons and property, and prevent crime. Specifically, it lacked the unifying hand of a single energetic commander. Such an individual would have the duty to study the habits of suspicious types and the power to interpose the law between honorable citizens and men of perverse instincts. "Without a head that can think and command, and without instruments that blindly execute, it is not possible to have any collective force, capable of ordered movements."

Proper police were idealized in this essay as men of blameless moral conduct, recognized personal courage, basic education, and intelligence. Such individuals could establish law and order, if appropriate remuneration were forthcoming. "There are always men competent to organize and command a worthy gendarmerie, giving it the military basis that we have indicated; among us no other basis is suitable."[45]

This seemed the opportune time to complete reform of the public service, which had been initiated in the police force in 1864. According to La semana, "Today what is happening with regard to petty thefts is truly scandalous: there are various families that notoriously exercise robbery as a profession, with incredible cynicism and impudence; due to that, the few days in jail which is usually imposed on them is not effective." Recidivism among both men and women was so bad that frequently when an individual caught the thief in the act he would "apply a personal correction" rather than deliver him to judicial authorities. "Say what you will about whipping as a punishment, there are circumstances which can recommend it and even demand it. Where the prison lacks the means to be truly correctional, whether by means of labor for the prisoners, or by bread and water (régimen alimenticio) and solitary confinement; where there is not at hand another recourse for cutting deeply ingrained evil at the root . . . it is necessary to have recourse to the only remedy that can put an end to it."

If whipping were substituted for "nominal" incarceration, the article suggested, the petty thieves, fights, woundings, and scandals witnessed daily in the city would disappear. Enforcement of vagrancy laws would help also. "Who does not know of the pernicious effect on a moral public of a habit common in this city of hanging out on the street corners, sometimes in groups, sometimes alone?" *La semana* asked. The police should break up this pattern. To the editorialist, "the circles of gamblers whom all the world sees daily" — from the street in front of the theatre to the outskirts of town — spelled trouble. Other danger signs were the bearing of illegal arms and the corruption, notably public drunkenness, coming from gambling houses and brothels. "In sum, reorganization of the police and severe repression of crimes are matters that justifiably preoccupy the public today and that demand preferential attention on the part of the authority charged with watching out for public tranquillity."[46]

Statistics, Exhibitions, and Schools

Although such semiofficial comments on law and order seem freighted with tradition, the Cerna regime throughout its tenure promoted more modern-sounding solutions to other problems. Statistics, for example, were viewed as the universal solvent of obstacles to Guatemala's development. In such areas as agricultural policy, this seemed a purely practical approach. It is clear, however, that to members of the elite, statistics should do more than enumerate comparative crop production. Repeatedly, editors expressed frank curiosity as to the meaning of both extended statistics and short-run or anecdotal data. They wanted to collect as many as possible and squeeze all the meaning they could from them. In April 1866 *La semana* expressed delight at a forty-six-page pamphlet of statistics put out by the city council covering virtually every institution in the municipality. The editor believed this to be the first time the city had gathered and published such data.[47]

Reports by hospitals were held to be particularly sensitive indicators of the condition and morality of the community: "The proportion between the sick and the wounded is a statistical datum of crime. . . . In the last year, according to . . . the annual report, the proportion of wounded to the sick was 14% of the men and 5% of the women." *La semana*'s editor noted that the report compares the five-year period 1819–1823 with the period 1863–1867 by comparing the number of wounded to the number of sick men for each of the ten years. The wounded ranged between 29.66% and 23% of the total sick for the earlier period and between 18.75% and 14% for the later one. The editor was particularly intrigued by the fact that the percentage for 1867 was the lowest (14%) and that in that year twenty-one murders were recorded in the city, whereas in the first three months of 1868, there had been fourteen murders already. "In three months the morality of the people could not have worsened, and the police were neither better nor worse than in the previous year." Probing further, he concluded that he did not know what these phenomena meant. Yet he could not resist noting that the city of Antigua in 1867 had proportions of wounded to sick of 38% for men and 20% for women. The following year an editor — perhaps the same individual — noted with relish that compared to the twenty-one murders in Guatemala City in 1867, there had been only fifteen in 1868, with only one occurring in the last nine months that year.[48]

Such concern with statistics blended two vital interests of the regime, one economic and one political. A policy of relatively scientific development of agriculture, the country's basic industry, had to be founded on data, and agricultural statistics were some of the earliest collected in Guatemala. Before the death of Carrera, they had already demonstrated the relative dynamism of coffee and stagnation of cochineal. Under Cerna they illustrated the mounting dominance of coffee and the further growth of the Pacific ports of San José, San Luís, and Champerico.[49]

To separate economic and political statistics neatly is sometimes difficult; one finds many economic figures that, when combined with social ones, might be considered political. From 1865 to 1870, the need for data was expressed like a drumbeat in the official press. Governments in Guatemala City always had particular difficulty persuading the corregidors — the officers in charge of the outlying provinces — to gather information in standard fashion. In the 1860s corregidors reported on their departments early each calendar year. In January 1866 the official *Gaceta* made clear that these reports were important in the making of government policy and that the data contained therein should be accurate if the government was to deal with reality. Furthermore, a government spokesman stated precisely what the data should reveal: (1) What moral and material progress was made in the year? (2) What most needed to be done in the following year? and (3) What specific means must be used to fulfill that need? He called for a statistical picture of the increase or decrease of plantings, production, commodity prices, crimes, convictions, population, revenues, students, schools, and public works. Periodically the *Gaceta* analyzed the statistics actually presented in a corregidor's report.[50]

Again, the argument for a wider and more thorough use of numerical data was pressed continuously in the late 1860s. In December 1866 Enrique Palacios provided a broader intellectual argument to the junta that governed the Economic Society: "Statistics are not in any way foreign to the work of our corporation, having as an object the exact knowledge of society considered in its nature, its elements, its economy, its situation and its movements.... [To] accomplish this ... statistical studies have been given a prominent place in modern societies." Palacios was particularly interested in regularizing collection of data on population changes in order to establish a demography for the country. Church data could be used by provincial officials in this pursuit, so Palacios furnished them a form for doing it, and three months later he provided the junta an update on the process.[51]

Such fascination with statistics had not weakened by 1870, when the *Gaceta* commented on the city's latest numerical report, indicating in no uncertain terms that this kind of data was what Guatemala needed for progress. The techniques used in the report were considered a step toward establishment of an effective population census. Cultural diversity of the population and fears of the military draft had forced the census to be taken by means of approximate calculations, but such obstacles would disappear in time.[52]

In October 1870 the Economic Society asked its members in the provinces to report regularly certain data to help with economic and social planning. The Society wanted to help the country advance, but, it noted, members in the outlying areas rarely corresponded with the leadership. It would help immensely if they would now change that pattern by sending agricultural information on a regular basis. Long before the geographical concept of "microclimates" was invented, their reality was recognized in Guatemala. The rainy season in 1879 was a case in point: Excessive rains occurred near Guatemala City even as drought destroyed grain crops in Zacapa, seventy miles away. With this in mind, leaders of the Society thought meteorological records should be kept not just in Guatemala City but also in each of the departments. The country needed all kinds of statistical reporting, starting with the meteorological, agricultural, and educational data. "We hope our corresponding members in the Departments will take our frank remarks in good spirit and cooperate, supporting our motto: united zeal creates abundance."[53]

One factor that encouraged emphasis on comparative data in the late 1860s was that economic figures were improving. A report of the municipal corporation of Guatemala City compared revenues and expenditures for the years 1863 to 1867 and found that annual revenues for 1867 were 11,000 pesos greater than in 1863. National export figures for 1866, 1867, and 1868 were similarly encouraging. Increased exports were noted for coffee, sugar, wool, rubber, and cochineal, even if there were a few declines (for commodities such as anise, rice, leathers, and cacao). Total exports were calculated at $1,870,091 for 1866, $1,996,450 for 1867, and over $2 million for 1868. The *Gaceta's* editor exulted at the rather modest figures: "We have here irrefutable proof of the movement for progress experienced by the Republic. . . . Let us hope that such auspicious progression will be seen in subsequent years."[54]

All of the charitable institutions, the judiciary, and especially the educational institutions yielded statistical reports, and the government's unfailing editorial response in those years was one of gratitude and the desire for more.

In another effort to promote progress, the Economic Society organized an annual national exhibition for agriculture, industry, and the fine arts. Inauguration of the Society's national museum in January 1866 was a preliminary step. The ceremony featured government ministers dedicating facilities and presenting achievement awards to students in the Society's free classes in mathematics and the fine arts. Organization of the museum had begun just two years earlier, but already its small collection of artifacts illustrated great interest in scientific classification and in national-scale exhibitions.[55]

In October 1866 the Society announced a general competition and exhibition of Guatemalan products, to open Christmas day. *La semana* noted that earlier exhibitions sponsored by the Society, though useful, had been very small. Exhibitions such as the one now announced would invite all products and producers of the country, a "noble" competition in full view of the consuming public, which could then compare the products freely. Competition and utility were to be the keynotes. "Such is the economic thought behind those formalities: they are not vain exhibitions of works more or less perfect; they are the arena in which the industrial, the artistic and the agricultural compete and learn." Competitors were urged to study features of previous winners and adapt them to their own entries. Products of general use and interest from regular industries should be emphasized over mere curiosities, *La semana* noted, and comprehensiveness should be the key. "The Corregidors and local authorities, parish priests, and members of the corporation are especially called to give zealous aid to . . . the project; the same should be said to all who desire the progress of the country, to see to it that the competition brings together the greatest possible number of agricultural products and works of art and of industry, so that it may produce the important results sought."[56] It was a major effort, and the establishment considered it a success.

The exhibition was repeated in succeeding years. Its opening in Christmas week 1868 was considered to be especially effective. The format and philosophy remained essentially unchanged: "We consider . . . that exposition to be a positive sign of the advance of the country, and the future toward which intelligence and patriotism are called, by means of work."[57] The *Gaceta* expressed satisfaction with an issue of the Society's journal devoted entirely to the successful 1868 event. This commentary seemed to send political, economic, and social signals, for along with the usual exercises in boosterism, it suggested that national maturity required the individual citizen to relate or connect affirmatively to the general good, and the government and corporations to establish a consistent line of conduct for the common welfare. "National expositions . . . are not simple acts of industrial vanity in countries accustomed to using them periodically. They amount to a judgment of *residencia* which peoples who desire advance and perfection take upon themselves. They compare yesterday with today in order to stimulate their progress and to dictate in full view of the results of their civilized action the measures necessary to develop their industry." The report on the exposition praised the corregidors of Izabal, Totonicapán, and San Marcos for contributing their services to it. Other corregidors were told they should do likewise.[58]

Discussion of public education was continuous from 1865 to 1870, but reforms were slight, the most notable being perhaps a greater emphasis on the teaching of English. Expansion of activities and facilities was more significant and included the opening of an industrial training school, reorganization of institutions such as the San Francisco school for poor children, grammar school scholarships for poor boys interested in the priesthood, and construction of a new building for the theological seminary. Discussion of curriculum during those years revealed much about the goals of the Cerna administration, and a conservative defense of the university statute revealed the regime's worldview with particular clarity. Noting the failed educational reform of the federation period (1824–1839), an experience dismissed as unrealistic and unsupported, a government spokesman criticized recent proposals to modernize the statute of the university. He favored the existing statute, written in 1840 after the triumph of the Carrera revolt and revised in 1855. In these two legislative actions, "the ancient statutes of 1686 were taken as the basis of organization of the University, the same that were in use in 1821." He added that only minor changes had been made since 1855.[59]

The spokesman continued, "To some it has seemed bad that the basis for the prime literary establishment of the country was found in a statute emitted nearly two hundred years earlier. For ourselves, we consider such criticism unjust and shallow, even if it is made in good faith. We covet progress in the country's letters as much as anyone. . . . Propagation of the sciences and the extension of ample public instruction, liberally and solidly founded, is of greatest importance." Why would maintenance of the old statute be an obstacle to such a goal? Before independence, the University of Guatemala reached a high degree of advancement and earned a reputation inside and outside the Realm of Guatemala under the 1686 code, producing men "consummate" in both ecclesiastical and natural sciences and in both civil and canon law. "Omitting that circumstance . . . universities are, by their nature, the institutions called *to conserve the ancient traditions in matters of science and teaching*, not in a blind spirit of routine but with that conservative, enlightened thought that accepts the new when it is good, but takes care to maintain the old when it is of some utility" (emphasis added).

Why did those who attacked the old university statute ignore the fact that the most celebrated universities in Europe "are preserved across time and from innovations, with their primitive physiognomy, even with the costumes and ceremonies that were established hundreds of years before, truly eminent men of sciences and letters defending those establishments against the innovating spirit?" One did not have to worship the ideas of the past to say that the constitution of 1686 was not at fault for the obvious problems of the university. Rather, disruptions caused by the wars for independence and the shifting policies that followed, compounded by inadequate funding, should be blamed. Perfectionism was not the answer.[60]

The government interested itself in direct and detailed management of the schools. In part this emphasis resulted from the small literate community in Guatemala, which traditionally had provided a tiny social arena in which to satisfy the appetite for pomp and circumstance. The academic community everywhere has always provided opportunities for public ceremony; it can always furnish an audience and an occasion. The fact that President Cerna chose to demonstrate both his piety and concern for youth by attending final examinations (mostly public and oral) at the Jesuit seminary will be understood immediately by any student or practitioner of politics. That he would hand out prize medals to top performers and that "one of the seminarians read an Ode in beautiful Castilian verses in honor of His Excellency the President" is also unremarkable.[61]

But the fact that the rector of the university required a decree from the government to alter the curriculum in advanced Latin and rhetoric tells something about the hermetic quality of the regime. The rector found it inconvenient that these courses were prerequisites for science courses and recommended that they be moved to the first and second year of the philosophy curriculum. This transfer was made in a government decree changing the arrangements previously decreed in 1859. (In a related illustration, statutes of the law school published in their entirety in the *Gaceta* in 1868 included detailed legal rules not only for law students' behavior but even for their demeanor.)[62]

The importance of instruction in rhetoric had been emphasized by a lengthy harangue in *La semana* several months earlier. "The study of Rhetoric . . . is the art of the well said" and hence necessary to civilized discourse. "Form is in many cases as necessary as substance." Some schools were seen to be doing a good job in this regard, but others were urged to pay attention to the admonition. These attitudes went hand in hand with sentiments expressed about term examinations at the Jesuit academy in late November 1869. "The maintenance of public order and respect for law and the authorities, which are supported by Guatemalans for the good of the republic, also help . . . to advance public instruction which fortunately is found today in quite promising condition in Guatemala."[63]

Indian Policy

It is clear that the Guatemalan elite was firmly conservative, even though it approved of progressive change. This consensus was buttressed by the conviction that various sectors of the population deserved lesser positions in the social structure. A major case in point was Indian policy, which fit the aristocratic/conservative outlook of the elite in almost geometrically complementary fashion. Though various Indian groups in Guatemala complained about their treatment, no dissent from existing policy could be found in the press of the capital.

During the earlier period of liberal dominance, the method of liberating Indians had been to remove colonial restrictions and to downgrade the traditional Church. The lower classes' response had been the *montañeses* revolt led by Carrera. That revolt and subsequent comment upon it tended to blur the distinction between Indians and ladinos in Guatemala. Distinction between the two groups was important, however, because of the different legal regime Indians had lived under during the Spanish colonial period — the regime that had been partly and temporarily lifted by the liberals in the 1820s and 1830s. Under Carrera, conservatives in league with the Church had reinstituted the Spanish colonial policy toward

Indians. A decree by the constitutional assembly issued on August 16, 1839, established a modified version of the Recopilación, the Spanish colonial legal code of 1686, as it applied to the Indians. A major feature of the colonial regime had been that different groups were treated differently before the law. The modernizing liberal regime eliminated by Carrera had tried to institute equal standing before the law.

In 1867 the *Gaceta* ridiculed once more such a "leveling" effort. It noted that following the 1839 renaissance of the Recopilación, features designed to "protect" the Indians had been sharpened (in 1851) to insist specifically that they must have a fixed residence in their community. As in colonial times, the corregidors were explicitly ordered to keep the Indians living in their proper villages (*reducciones*), not scattered about in the mountains. The Indians must be taught to use Spanish in order to achieve at least minimal communication with official society. Finally, the corregidor was expected to visit the villages in his department regularly in order to discharge the government's obligations to the Indians, who were seen mainly as wards of the state. Some of this view applied to rural peasants of whatever racial mixture, and it required an aristocratic interpretation: "We . . . insist . . . that the protection which is ordered to be given to said class [Indians] should never be interpreted against them. This is a point of major importance, and the same laws to which we have referred, wise and farseeing under many concepts, certainly do not leave this to the freewill of everyone. It cannot be said that there is protection for the indigenes in the undue tolerance of their faults."[64]

After the unsuccessful revolt of Serapio Cruz in 1867, the tone of official philosophy mellowed slightly. Celebration of President Cerna's birthday, aside from eliciting the usual compliments, brought explicit satisfaction at unified oligarchic authority. Stated the *Gaceta*: "It is satisfactory to observe on occasions like this the union of *all the persons to whom are commended the direction of public business in its diverse branches*, and to observe how each day the respect for authority has continued to be strengthened. . . . Today all understand that this principle is the main basis of order; and that without it, there is no stability in institutions, nor progress, nor true liberty; since these qualities (*bienes*) are preserved and developed in the shadow of a benign, just and protective authority" (emphasis added).[65]

In January 1869 a presidential election commission of the Chamber of Deputies made an exhortation for peace to conserve the nation's strength and called for leadership by the most enlightened part of society, "which serves as guide for the masses (*muchedumbre*) lingering in moral and intellectual infancy." The historic upheavals in Guatemala and other Latin American countries were cited as useful lessons in that regard.[66]

By June 1869 commissions were preparing reports on such important matters as the best use of the loan contracted in England and the renegotiation of financial relations with El Salvador. These commissions illustrated the importance the government placed on unity in light of the developing political crisis of that year. The *Gaceta* remarked, "The government has shown repeatedly that it desires the cooperation of all intelligent and patriotic citizens; it wishes that all take part in that which is of interest to all. Thus, without prejudice to consultation with the Council of State on important affairs, there are created from time to time commissions of competent persons, whose cooperation is as useful to the government, as it is honorific for those who serve."[67]

Having argued since 1867 that every effort had been made to share governance with the elite, whom it held by every test to provide the proper leaders of the country, the government insisted finally that it had developed a humane and graceful stance that would be attractive to civilized foreign visitors. "The sentiments of charity which honor men so much, are the most brilliant introduction by which they can present themselves to their fellow creatures." The foreign traveler in any country must judge its culture in significant part by what it does to relieve human pain. "For the man who abounds in sentiments of philanthropy the great moments which embellish a nation, however attractive to other observers, are of less interest than the modest house in which youth receive a free education, of the hospital in which the indigent find a remedy for their ills, or of the refuge which feeds the destitute child and the unhappy old person who without that resource could perish victims of nakedness and misfortune." Guatemala City, through its charitable establishments, could now expect a favorable judgment by the foreigner. Quetzaltenango furnished another instance of charity as civilization: It had a good hospital that had improved greatly during the two preceding years. A columnist was quite sure that such "institutions of charity and mercy are seen everywhere as a sure index of culture and civilization.[68]

Although the Cerna administration invited all men of good will and qualifications to share the hard thinking on questions of governance, it was not guilty of utopianism — if any could have thought that. The question always arose whether the state was obligated "to exercise acts of piety" for the poor and unfortunate in its territory. The question was subjected to lengthy juridical argument, with the conclusion that "preventive measures against poverty have application in all times and places. Alms have their place and their limits; to give them is to commit an act of piety, as in principle it is an act of prodigality; and governments do not have the right to be prodigal, because they do not administer [their own money and] because the nation wishes to profit from what it gives. In sum, societies motivate their members that they should be worthy and hardworking."[69]

Notes

1. For contemporary formulation of the generalization about Central America, cf. "Las discusiones políticas y las mejoras intelectuales, morales y materiales," *La semana* I, 95 (November 19, 1866); re rivers, cf. Ralph Lee Woodward, Jr., *Class Privilege and Economic Development: The Consulado de Comercio of Guatemala, 1793–1871* (Chapel Hill: University of North Carolina Press, 1966), 94.

2. Pio Casals (pseudonym for Enrique Palacios), *Reseña de la situación general de Guatemala, 1863*, Edición, introducción y notas por Jorge Lujan Muñoz (Guatemala: Academia de Geografía e Historia de Guatemala, 1981; 1st ed., 1865), 2–3.

3. The advanced literary character of the geographically isolated Guatemala City elite is reflected in the general quality of publications there in the 1860s. The group's character is best illustrated not by the more famous intellectuals such as José Milla (nom de plume, Salomé Jil), Miguel García Granados, or the formidable Colombian emigré Mariano Ospina, but by a popular military man, Field Marshal José Víctor Zavala. Zavala became a preeminent dissident under Cerna, and his European literary interests were not limited to the Spain of his immediate forebearers but included his translation of a literary work from the German to the Spanish: "El desquite, cuento, escrito en alemán por Francisco Hoffman y traducido al castellano, por J. Víctor Zavala," *La semana* I, 91 (October 14, 1866), 3–4, as the fourth installment of a serialized printing that ran at least through number 95 (November 19, 1866).

4. "La muerte del General Carrera, I," *La semana* I, 18 (April 30, 1865), 1.

5. "El manifiesto del Excmo. Sr. Presidente de la republica," *La semana* I, 22 (May 3, 1865), 1.

6. *La semana* I, 30 (June 30, 1865), 1; *Gaceta* XIV, 78 (July 12, 1865); "Atentado contra el comisionado de Guatemala en Nicaragua," 80 (July 22, 1865), 7; "El Sr. Palacios," 87 (September 9, 1865), 6. See also F. Hernandez de León, *El libro de Efemérides. capítulos de la historia de la America Central*, III (Guatemala: 1930), 77–81, 391–398. For U.S. reports on Barrios's capture, Andrew Dickenson, León, No. 107, July 8, 1865, FM 219, R 14, and on his execution, James Partridge to Henry Seward, San Salvador, No. 68, December 3, 1865, FM 219, R 23.

7. "Elección de presidente constitucional de la república," La semana I, 19 (May 7, 1865), 1.

8. Reunión de la cámara de representantes, *La semana* I, 47 (November 26, 1865), 1; cf. "Las discusiones políticas y las mejoras intelectuales, morales y materiales," and 95 (November 19, 1866). See also John R. Gillis, *The Development of European Society*,

1770–1870 (New York: Houghton Mifflin, 1977, and Lanham, MD: University Press of America, 1983), 84–85, on the theme of sanscullotism vs. elitism.

9. "Fin del año; nuestra publicación," *La semana* I, 52 (December 31, 1865), 1.

10. "La autoridad y el progreso social," *La semana* I, 53 (January 8, 1866).

11. "República de Salvador, indicaciones," *La semana* I, 77 (June 24, 1866), 1.

12. "Centro-América," *La semana* I, 80 (July 16, 1866), 1.

13. Comment, *La semana* I, 54 (January 14, 1866), 2. The uprising of small landholders of African descent at Morant Bay, Jamaica, in October 1865 saw the burning of the courthouse and much of the town and the killing of at least eighteen persons. Governor Edward Eyre's government executed more than three hundred persons in putting down the revolt and claimed this to be exemplary justice. Liberals in England were outraged. The incident triggered the end of legislative government (dominated by the merchant and planter class) in Jamaica and the introduction of the authoritarian Crown Colony government, not only in Jamaica but in most of the British West Indies.

14. "La guerra entre España y algunas repúblicas sudamericanas," *La semana* I, 72 (May 20, 1866), 1.

15. Untitled editorial, *La semana* I, 100 (January 13, 1867), 1.

16. "Repúblicas hispano-americanas," *La semana* II, 10 (May 7, 1867), 1.

17. "Los gobiernos," *La semana* II, 96 (April 11, 1869), 1; "Las discusiones políticas y las mejoras intelectuales, morales y materiales," I, 95 (November 19, 1866), 1; "Consideraciones generales," II, 98 (April 25, 1866), 1.

18. "La paz," *La semana* I, 61 (March 4, 1866), 1.

19. "La falta de noticias," *La semana* I, 73 (May 27, 1866), 1.

20. "Centro-América; revista para el exterior," *La semana* I, 78 (July 1, 1866).

21. "El espíritu conservador y el de reforma; consideraciones históricas, III," *La semana* II, 30 (September 23, 1867).

22. "El espíritu conservador y el de reforma; consideraciones históricas, IV," *La semana* II, 31 (October 10, 1867), 1. N. B., this interpretation ignores the violent period in Chile before 1829 when radical reform was attempted.

23. "Los gobiernos," *La semana* II, 96 (April 11, 1869), 1.

24. Woodward, *Class Privilege*, 81–104.

25. "El comercio de la república," *La semana* I, 49 (December 11, 1865), 1; "Caminos," *Gaceta* XV, 5 (February 7, 1866), 37.

26. "Caminos," *Gaceta* XV, 8 (March 6, 1866).

27. Salvador Cobos and Vicente Zebadua, April 8, 1866, to Junta de Gobierno de Consulado, *Gaceta* XV, 15 (May 16, 1866), 114–115.

28. P. N. Sánchez a Junta de Gobierno, May 3, 1866, *Gaceta* XV, 15 (May 16, 1866), 115–117.

29. Ministerio de Gobernación, Decreto de concesión para construir un ferro-carril entre la villa de Escuintla y el puerto de San José, *Gaceta* XV, 70 (February 14, 1868), 558–559; "Riqueza de la república," *Gaceta* XVI, 6 (February 25, 1869), 3. Official hopes for a railroad from Guatemala City to San José on the Pacific went back at least to 1858. The Anglo-Guatemala treaty of 1859 contained, in its notorious Article 7, a British commitment to aid construction of a cart road from the north (Caribbean) coast to the capital — a route over which it had been difficult to maintain even a good horse trail. So despite the desires of coffee planters, little had been accomplished toward export routes, and a traditional frame of reference remained strong in regard to the rest of the road system.

30. *Ibid.*

31. "Empréstito," *Gaceta* XVI, 14 (April 27, 1869), 4; "Inversión del Empréstito," *Gaceta* XVI, 20 (June 13, 1869), 2.

32. "Ferrocarril del norte," *Gaceta* XVI, 65 (April 26, 1870), 3–4; Corregidor de Izabal, Informe, June 1, 1870, *Gaceta* XVI, 73 (June 21, 1870), 3–5; Consulado de Comercio (Antonio Machado, Enrique Palacios, T. Valenzuela, and Ricardo Casanova [Síndico]), "Caminos," *Sociedad económica* II, 11 (December 15, 1870), 86–87, and 12 (December 31, 1870), 92–93.

33. Woodward, *Class Privilege*, 60–80.

34. Ministerio de lo interior, *Gaceta* XV, 21 (July 14, 1866), 165–166; "Muelle de San José," *Gaceta* XV, 21 (July 14, 1866), N. B. contract articles 3, 7, 9, and 11 on concessions; cf. Ministerio de gobernación, Memorandum sobre . . . la erección de muelles en la Costa del Pacífico, *Gaceta* XV, 45 (May 11, 1867), 359–363.

35. *Gaceta* XV, 57 (September 6, 1867), 455; "Muelle de San José," *Gaceta* XV, 82 (July 23, 1868), 653.

36. "Correos" and "Hospital de San Juan de Diós," *Gaceta* XVI, 40 (November 4, 1869), 2.

37. "Telégrafos submarinos," *Gaceta* XV, 49 (June 15, 1867), 391; O. du Teil, director, anuncio, "Companía de los telégrafos de Guatemala," *Gaceta* XV, 6 (October 27, 1867), 491. See also "Telégrafo intercontinental," *Gaceta* XV, 66 (January 3, 1868), 528–529, an inspirational essay on progress extracted from *La república* (Santiago, Chile).

38. "El telégrafo," *La semana* II, 52 (May 7, 1868), 1; Telégrafo, Aviso al público, *Gaceta* XV, 80 (July 3, 1868), 644.

39. Consulta del Consejo de Estado, acuerdos del Gobierno y communicación del Ilmo. Sr. Arzobispo sobre la cuestión de propiedad de la Plazuela del Sagrario, y sobre creación de un mercado público en ella, *Gaceta* XV, 14 (May 9, 1866), 105–106.

40. David Luna, "Higiene pública; mercado de la Plaza del Sagrario," *Sociedad económica* I, 6 (August 1866), 122–126, 127 (plan); see also "Cuestión de actualidad," *La semana* I, 71 (May 13, 1866), 1. The cliche: "Dime lo que comes, te diré lo que eres."

41. Anuncios, "Construcción del mercado en la Plaza del Sagrario," *Gaceta* XVI, 32 (September 7, 1869), 6.

42. "Mercado de Cerna," *Gaceta* XVI, 39 (October 27, 1869), 1; Orsini Juslongo, "La alimentación pública," *Sociedad económica* II, 8 (October 31, 1870), 57.

43. Acuerdo . . . , *Gaceta* XV, 3 (January 20, 1866), 18; "Reforma de las carceles de la capital," *La semana* I, 55 (January 21, 1866); "La cárcel," *La semana* I, 82 (July 30, 1866), 1.

44. "La cárcel," *La semana* I, 82 (July 30, 1866), 1.

45. "Policía de seguridad," *La semana* II, 47 (March 20, 1868), 1.

46. *Ibid.*

47. "Memoria del Ayuntamiento de la capital," *La semana* I, 69 (April 29, 1866), 1.

48. "Hospitales — estadística del crimen," *La semana* II, 50 (April 21, 1868), 1; "Hospital general," *Gaceta* XVI, 7 (March 2, 1869), 3–4.

49. "Agricultura," *Gaceta* XV, 76 (May 13, 1868), 610; "Crédito pública," *Gaceta* XV, 4 (January 29, 1866); "Comercio de la república in 1865," *Gaceta* XV, 16 (May 26, 1866). See also proposal for agricultural archive, Cámara de representantes, Sesión . . . 11 de enero de 1867, *Gaceta* XV, 41 (March 21, 1867), 325.

50. "Informes de los corregidores," *Gaceta* XV, 2 (January 12, 1866), 2–3; "Informe del correjimiento de Guatemala," *Gaceta* XV, 13 (April 30, 1866), 100; "Informe del correjidor de Izabal," *Gaceta* XV, 73 (April 3, 1868).

51. Enrique Palacios, "Estadística," *Sociedad económica* I, 8 (December 1866); Palacios, "Estadística," *Sociedad económica* I, 10 (March 1867), 186–187.

52. "Estadística de la capital," *Gaceta* XVI, 55 (February 19, 1870), 3.

53. "Los departamentos y la Sociedad Económica," *Sociedad económica* II, 7 (October 15, 1870). See also comment on questionnaire of Sociedad Económica in *Gaceta* XVI, 13 (April 16, 1869), 5.

54. "Municipalidad," *Gaceta* XV, 74 (April 18, 1868), 594; "Exportaciones," *Gaceta* XV, 78 (June 4, 1868), 626; "Comercio de exportación," *Gaceta* XVI, 25 (July 21, 1869), 1.

55. "Sociedad económica," *Gaceta* XV, 3 (January 20, 1866), 18–19.

56. "Exhibición," *La semana* I, 91 (October 14, 1866), 1. For a lengthy description, cf. "Sociedad económica," *Gaceta* XV, 36 (January 28, 1867), 289.

57. Anuncios, Exhibición de la Sociedad Económica, *Gaceta* XV, 90 (September 29, 1868), 730–731.

58. "La exhibición nacional de 1868," *Gaceta* XVI, 9 (March 18, 1869), 5–6. The philosophy of national exhibitions is spelled out in the report of the Sociedad Económica, *Gaceta* XVI, 15 (May 4, 1869), 16 (May 12, 1869), and 17 (May 22, 1869). N. B., *residencia* in the Spanish empire was a period of residence routinely required of an outgoing official while his term of office was reviewed for possible misconduct.

59. "Colegio clerical de San Vicente de Paul," *Gaceta* XV, 26 (September 11, 1866); "Instrucción pública, I," *La semana* I, 56 (January 28, 1866), 1. Other installments of this major series on education at 57 (February 4, 1866), 58 (February 11, 1866), and 60 (February 26, 1866).

60. "Instrucción pública, II" *La semana* I, 57 (February 4, 1866), 1.

61. "Colegio seminario," *La semana* I, 94 (November 11, 1866), 1.

62. Acuerdo alterando la época para el curso de estudios de latinidad superior y de retórica, *Gaceta* XV, 12 (April 19, 1866, 89–90; Decreto aprobando los estatutos del colegio de abogados, *Gaceta* XV, 78 (June 4, 1868), 621.

63. "Instrucción pública; colegio seminario," *Gaceta* XVI, 42 (November 16, 1869), 1–2.

64. "Indígenas, I–II," *Gaceta* XV, 36 (January 28, 1867), 288–289; "Indígenas, V–VI," 38 (February 16, 1867), 305–306; "Indígenas, VII–VIII," 39 (February 24, 1867), 311.

65. "Del Exmo. Señor Presidente," *Gaceta* XV, 68 (January 26, 1868), 544.

66. Cámara de representantes, *Gaceta* XV, 100 (January 7, 1869), 797.

67. "Comisiones," *Gaceta* XVI, 21 (June 19, 1869), 3.

68. "Beneficencia; hospital de Quetzaltenango," *Gaceta* XVI, 24 (July 13, 1869).

69. "La caridad legal," *Gaceta* XVI, 29 (August 16, 1869), 5–6.

3

Contradictions, 1865–1870

To a remarkable degree, old Spain lived on in Guatemala in the 1860s. The Cerna administration, representing an elite consensus, extended in time a conservative regime based upon the traditional values and institutions of the Spanish empire. Yet this government was committed to modernizing the country enough to develop economically. Indeed, economic development came very close to its definition of progress — "true progress," as the government called it. But some persons who sought power or redress in the years following Carrera's death dissented from the government. Some in the Chamber of Deputies thought it ridiculous to use antique autocratic institutions as instruments to achieve modernity, and not all of Carrera's old peasant allies felt included. Finally, able and educated foreigners attracted by the coffee industry were interested in government cooperation and efficiency, not in the traditional Hispanic way of life treasured so ostentatiously by the Guatemala City elite.

One symbol of the regime's limitations was the *estanco*, a monopoly franchise granted by the government for some commodity or service. It characterized those Spanish imperial devices for delegating power that were still basic to the conservative state. Similarly, the Roman Catholic Church had a monopoly of religion, and its presence was so pervasive that one could not measure its limits. The Consulado de Comercio, a monopoly structure for merchants, carried out many quasi-governmental operations, such as operation of the commercial court and maintenance of roads. Most professions and industries had their own tribunals; thus, in fact and by charter, citizens were not necessarily equal before the law. As in colonial times, the medical profession was licensed under the Protomedicato. Indian villages were referred to as *reducciones*, as they had been since the sixteenth century, when Indians had been rounded up and forced to live under Spanish jurisdiction. The provincial administrator, or *jefe político*, was still called *corregidor*, as in Hapsburg times. Seventeenth-century laws were still routinely cited as the current law code, and not just in Indian affairs. However, as an everyday reminder of privilege, the estanco probably made the ordinary citizen highly conscious of discrimination.

In terms of government revenue, the most important estanco in the nineteenth century was the one that controlled the manufacture and sale of alcoholic beverages, primarily *aguardiente* and *chicha*. Aguardiente is a clear liquor (rum) distilled from fermented cane sugar; chicha is a local fermented drink, usually corn beer. In 1865 the monopoly for these products was auctioned off in various provinces, in effect to private agents for the government (*arrendadores*). Citing the law code of Castile, the Guatemalan regulating statute exhorted all concerned (generally the owners and operators of stills) that the arrendadores must be avid in collecting all taxes due, without discounts. Natural or human disasters could be no excuse.[1]

A year later the Cerna regime attempted to modernize this basic revenue source by spreading interest in the estanco to a larger group of investors. The monopoly was now placed in the hands of a new, private corporation. Both distillers and sugar producers were urged to invest in it. The corporation was formed in the summer of 1866 with capital of 500,000 pesos represented by 1,000 shares of 500 pesos each.[2] The company's statute was lengthy, laid out in six titles and forty-seven articles. This device seemed to be part of a major effort to satisfy the interests of sugar planters, coffee planters, and any other provincial/rural capitalists who felt they had an interest in the liquor tax. Apparently, some considered it a dirty business. One Vicente de la Hoz, listed in the *Gaceta* as a shareholder, wrote the editor insisting that it be announced that he was *not* a shareholder.[3]

In his annual message, President Cerna expressed some pride in the new arrangement, pointing to the seven-year lease "of the estancos de aguardientes to a company of capitalists and proprietors of fincas of sugar cane that is formed for that purpose. The concession of a license for the production and sale of *licores estancados* to an association which includes many who might have worked against the monopoly is a positive advance." The concessionary company was to pay the government annually 100,000 pesos more than the estancos had paid the previous year. It would thus produce nearly 400,000 pesos in revenue.[4] In August 1867 revised statutes of the company were published with the signatures of eighteen founders.

The company was to have its home office in Guatemala City, with branches and agencies at other points of the country. Urban-rural and capital-provincial tensions probably forced this resolution of the problem of an alcoholic beverages estanco. By making 500-peso shares available, the government provided an opportunity for a wider spectrum of investors, whether urban or rural.[5]

Its handling of other kinds of problems suggests that the Cerna regime generally tried to accommodate the power structure of the provinces, though frequently official publications obscured the facts of a particular situation. It was announced in September 1865, for instance, that "some disorders occurred in the pueblo of Santa Catarina Ixtahuacán [Department of Sololá] over local questions and differences among the residents of said town and its own authorities." A commission and a magistrate were sent to settle the matter and re-establish order among the Indians. This accomplished, the *Gaceta* concluded that all was well unless future "ulterior and unknown causes" disturbed the situation. According to the government, the settlement resulted from "its desire for the welfare of those Indians whose ignorance and miserable condition led them almost always to excesses and misconduct for reasons of little or no importance, with manifest prejudice to themselves." The facts in question were left unmentioned, but the statement's paternalism was manifest.

> The Government properly takes into account the present state of the indigenes, seeking in all circumstances to fulfill the laws dictated in their favor; but it desires also that they not be left to their own fate by a false interpretation of those legal arrangements. Thus, when the appropriate agency has stressed to higher authorities of Departments the good treatment which laws provide for the Indians, it ought not to be understood that the government wishes to allow them to act out their faults with impunity, even less that they be excused from observance of obligations appropriate to them under the same laws. Obligations must be fulfilled, and faults punished; but all with the prudence and consideration which the ancient laws foresaw, and which have been long mandated in the Republic. Those charged with the governance of Indian villages ought to adhere precisely to those laws.[6]

The president had personally approved of arrangements made by the commission for Santa Catarina, but the editorialist gave little hint of the actual circumstances. In fact, the magistrate's report indicates only that a dangerous situation of Indian disorder had been pacified through the cooperation of the power structures of Quetzaltenango, Totonicapán, and Sololá.[7]

Cruz and Rufino Barrios

For more than a year and a half after the police incident at Santa Catarina, civil order in the country went largely unchallenged, with only minor incidents occurring. Then, in early February 1867, the government reported that the old warhorse Serapio Cruz had gone into open rebellion. Because a state of emergency existed, the state suspended the civil guarantees of Articles 18 through 24 of the law of February 5, 1839, until order could be restored.[8] The Gaceta commented at length on the villainy of Cruz, the generosity of Cerna, and the lack of justification for revolt, observing that Cruz's movement was based on "petty personal considerations" and thus would not attract the solid villagers of the country. Such intrigues had become transparent because the people had learned more than the revolutionaries. Still, "every disturbance hurts, however small; interrupting businesses and imposing on the Government the need to employ for defense of authority and order resources destined for works of agriculture and of the arts. Those who promote disorder are responsible for all those evils, and they ought not to complain if the government, in compliance with its most sacred duties, proceeds with severity against all those who try to bring the horrors of war upon the country."[9]

From the first, the government painted this "seditious movement" by Cruz as a small affair. "With three or four members of his family, the servants of his hacienda and a few unwary people whom he had seduced, under specious pretext of claiming that he did not promote an insurrection against ... the President, Don Serapio Cruz placed himself in open rebellion against authority." In a dawn attack on the town of Guastatoya, he had taken eighteen army weapons stored in the local military headquarters. Appropriate forces under Generals Antonino and Gregorio Solares had been sent to the scene, and an interesting exchange of letters with Field Marshal Zavala announced Cruz's intentions.[10]

For the next month a stream of bulletins from the government followed the course of the rebellion to its defeat. On March 9 an editorial announced with satisfaction that the people had rejected the grossly unjustified call of Cruz and that the military's relentless pursuit had squelched the insurrection. Serapio Cruz had surrendered in Sanarate to a subordinate of General Antonino Solares. With the approval of the government, Cruz was exiled to El Salvador, agreeing not to return to Guatemala without permission. Pursuit had been so deft, it was boasted, that hardly a shot had been fired.[11]

Shortly the government announced that the extraordinary clemency shown Cruz would be extended to his followers, those officers and men who took part in the "suffocated" rebellion. The government and the Supreme Court agreed upon punishments: (1) loss of rank for three captains and six lieutenants; (2) exile to the Mexican state of Chiapas for four individuals, two of whom were members of the Cruz family; (3) confinement in the Petén, with freedom to leave the country, for four others; and, (4) assignment to Izabal, a hardship post, for eight persons, who were to serve at either the port of Livingston or the port of Santo Tomás.[12]

In mopping up the revolt, Cerna conducted some conciliatory personal diplomacy. In mid-April it was reported that the president had made a visit to the Indian villages of Mataquescuintla, Santa Rosa, and Cuajiniquilapa in the eastern mountains. "His Excellency dictated his measures for the best order of those *reducciones* and took other necessary steps for the good government of populations that he visited," the *Gaceta* wrote. "Everywhere he was received with demonstrations of respect and adhesion, finding the most decided desire to cooperate in the conservation of peace and maintenance of order." Cerna arranged for back pay for the battalion of Santa Rosa, offered aid to widows of the military, and even gave a small sum to the wife of one Basilio Pérez, who was confined to Izabal on the north coast for having taken an active part in the rebellion. Moreover, he gave aid to needy persons from his own pocket and offered to pay the cost of the altar of a chapel being built in Santo Domingo los Ocotes. This entire story was printed in boldface type on the first page of the *Gaceta*.[13]

The increasing involvement of Mexican authorities in Guatemalan insurrectionary politics was alarming, as was the appearance of the rebel José Rufino Barrios — his name later changed to Justo Rufino Barrios. A newspaper in Chiapas charged that Guatemalans were invading and occupying lands in Chiapas. Government spokesmen in Guatemala found it necessary to deny this allegation and to assert that quite the opposite was true.[14] This exchange occurred on the eve of the elimination of Maximilian of Hapsburg's Mexican empire and the full return to power of Benito Juárez — a perilous reversal for the conservative, pro-clerical regime of Cerna. The continuing problems of Cruz's revolt, Mexican boundary threats, and ideological contradictions all came together in the protean figure of Rufino Barrios as he stepped onto the historical stage in Central America. Wrote the *Boletín de noticias*, "On the hacienda called the Malacate, belonging to the notary Don Rufino Barrios, some twenty individuals have rendezvoused, the larger part of the [Guatemalan] exiles residing in the neighboring republic. The principal leaders were Francisco and Ramón Cruz [and] the same Rufino Barrios." (The two Cruzes were among those exiled to Chiapas the previous spring.)

The entire group left the Malacate on August 2 with Rufino Barrios in the lead. Barrios split off to carry out a recruiting mission while the others headed in the direction of San Marcos, taking provisions from farms in the vicinity. The next day, under the command of Francisco Cruz, this latter party was foraging for supplies when it came to the place called San Rafael Pie de la Cuesta. There it encountered two young men working their *fincas* (farms) and took from them their horses and weapons. The youths reported this incident to San Marcos and later headed for the town themselves. Unfortunately, the message — and then the farmers themselves — fell into the hands of Cruz, who had them shot. Cruz later rejoined Barrios to attack both San Marcos and San Pedro Sacatepéquez successfully before heading for Quetzaltenango.

Then the unexpected happened. "The seditionists learned that Brigadier Pacheco with a force from Quetzaltenango was [nearby]. They feared being overpowered and so dispersed, retreating by different routes. But the indigenes of San Pedro, who were hidden near the town, captured Francisco Cruz and Lázaro Bonilla and, successively as they came along, the others to the number of thirty seven, among them some of the leaders." These events, spurred by the surprising ferocity of the embattled villagers, led to the court-martial, conviction, and execution of Francisco Cruz. Not only was the uprising snuffed out, but almost all the arms taken in San Marcos were recovered.[15] The government found encouragement in the indignant action of the Indians of San Pedro, opposing and capturing a rebel against the regime. When Cerna addressed the Chamber of Representatives in late November, he recounted a good year and referred loftily to the attacks by Serapio Cruz, Francisco Cruz, and Rufino Barrios as "that slight restlessness, the work of a few ambitious men who cannot get along with any government which tries to conduct public business in an orderly way."[16]

These events that comforted Cerna brought a rhapsodic editorial from the *Gaceta*, which saw them as vindication. "Providence has favored the Republic . . . during the year just concluded. An insensate attempt to end the peace resulted only in affirming it, showing how diminished are those who seek disorder and how the great majority of citizens have decided to sustain an order that has assured the country's tranquility and established a basis for its welfare and growth." All groups were seen as working together under the established system to improve the country, put down troublemakers, and thus maintain the necessary peace. The editor noted the tranquil situation in the rest of Central America, in effect holding the Cruz revolt to be the exception that proved the rule.[17]

Not six months passed before a government bulletin announced that various exiles in Soconusco who had harassed the area around San Marcos were again attacking villages along the border: "The ringleader Rufino Barrios, one of those who accompanied Cruz in the attack of August 3 last year, escaped with various perverse types and located at his hacienda, the Malacate, from which he constantly threatens small frontier villages. The circumstances of this hacienda, part in Guatemala and part in Soconusco, has impeded pursuit of Barrios and those who accompany him." The most recent skirmish had occurred at Malacatán, where the attackers were beaten off after a hard rain destroyed their advantage. Reports indicated that the attackers left behind thirteen dead, several obsolete weapons, and a few horses, and that on his retreat Barrios attacked the aguardiente works in San Pablo. The reporter presumed that Barrios would soon be undone by border garrisons.[18]

García Granados

Cerna served almost four years as president under largely peaceful conditions. The only remotely credible threats to his regime had been the return to power of the liberal Juárez regime in Mexico and the revolt of Serapio Cruz in Guatemala. Since the Cruz revolt fell apart in a month with no evidence of popular support, only the Mexican regime, which broke off diplomatic relations, seemed ominous. However, as Cerna's presidential term approached its end, a serious civil political challenge materialized for the first time. Official sources of the regime tend to obscure the existence of political opposition, aside from cases of anarchy or insurrection. But one clear dissenter stands out in the political dialogue: Miguel García Granados (1809–1878). In 1865, after the Chamber of Representatives elected Cerna to succeed the late President Carrera, García Granados refused to sign the election certificate.[19] Because Carrera had been named president-for-life in 1854, there were differences of interpretation in the 1865 and 1869 presidential elections, the first attempted under the Acta Constitutiva of 1851.[20]

García Granados's dissent in the 1860s is mentioned in official publications only in formal political terms. One can deduce that he was the champion of democratic process in an oligarchic context. Looking behind those sources, he seems a logical representative of moderate liberalism. His family was entrenched in the commercial class in Guatemala and had been since it arrived from Cádiz, Spain, in January 1811. Even earlier his father, as a very young man, had done well trading in Guatemala; he returned to Spain in 1792, but the French occupation of Spain after 1808 caused him to emigrate to Guatemala with his growing family in 1811. Miguel had been born in Spain in 1809. By the 1820s the García Granados sons, living in a province of the disintegrating Spanish empire, had come to think of themselves as followers of Voltaire.[21] Miguel was a liberal until the triumph of Carrera, after which he became identified with the "left wing" of the conservatives. This meant he was an acceptable liberal. He also became an exceedingly popular professor in the university. Thus, he came naturally enough to his role as the great dissenter of the Cerna regime.[22]

García Granados's philosophy of reform was gradualist in character, matching that of the Cerna regime. The rhetoric of his memoirs, published in 1877, is remarkably similar to that found in the organs of the Cerna regime, La semana and the Gaceta. Only with regard to the Church did his agenda diverge from the state's. The Cerna regime was slavish in its obeisance to the religious hierarchy. Clearly García Granados was not, but to his dying day he thought it unlikely that any government in a Latin American country could be freed completely from Church influence. He insisted that reformers in Central America would have to take these realities into account.

García Granados believed the causes of the Carrera revolution explained its reactionary character. "After the ultraliberal party triumphed in 1829," he wrote, "it decided to diminish the influence and power of the clergy that was immense in Central America as in other Spanish countries, and it may even be said, in all Roman Catholic countries." Those reformers had not grasped the enormity of their task, nor had they the means to complete it. Reformers usually failed in history, including those in countries much more advanced than Central America. "Consider France, an enlightened and powerful nation, and one swarming with men eminent in all scientific and administrative areas. Although the reformers seemed quickly to achieve their object there and to destroy completely the power of the clergy, a clerical reaction occurred later, and now it is recognized that the influence believed lost was reborn with stubborn force, resisting the establishment of liberal institutions." There was much less religious fanaticism in France than "in ignorant and semibarbarous countries." Yet clerical influence had survived the reformers even there.

Reform always required generations to accomplish, and reformers got no thanks for their efforts. To García Granados it seemed inevitable that more than a few months would be required "to destroy an edifice whose construction took centuries." He thought the scientific axiom "nature does not function in leaps" could be applied to all social reforms, particularly those aimed at religious habits. Despite this pessimism he thought leaders should not avoid making necessary reforms just because there were obstacles. Such behavior would be cowardly. "What I wish to teach is that in order for reforms to be solid, and not to provoke the atrocious reactions that always set countries back, diverting them for many years from the correct road which they had approached carelessly, it is indispensable to make them march with slow, firm, prudent step." Government should know its objectives, survey the obstacles carefully, and proceed deliberately. "To direct a country as our reformers did from 1829 to 1837, is to throw it to chance, and to show a complete lack of statesmanship."[23]

In the 1860s both the *Gaceta* and *La semana*, representing the government, called for and appealed to an elite consensus that included conservatives and liberals but excluded "foreign" liberal doctrine. Conversely, García Granados saw definite value in non-Hispanic secular theory if it were applied gradually, incrementally, and with due regard to local realities. This belief was demonstrated in his parliamentary activity in the late 1860s and again in his memoirs. He chose the development of Britain's parliamentary system as the model of gradualism in action. "Tact and prudence do not imply a lack of resolution. Proceeding in this manner, progress is secure and constant. Each step that is taken, each stairstep that is climbed, there is no fear of retracing it, or turning to descent, the process making retrocession impossible." If, however, a nation tried to "travel by leaps," some of those leaps would be taken in the dark, and the country would risk crashing into unforeseen obstacles. That, he argued, is what happened to Guatemala's reformers in 1829, who had read theory but lacked experience. "England, for two centuries now, has made immense reforms in its political organization and even in the religious. That nation has had a complete transformation of its institutions and in the spirit of its legislation; but this transformation has been verified step by step. Each reform was discussed for many years; and when the majority of the nation was persuaded, it was accepted and decreed." In that way peaceful change had been accomplished, and England was now admired by all foreigners who took the trouble to study it.

It should be emphasized that García Granados advocated the purposeful gradualism he found in British history but did not always agree with the mechanics of the British political system. Dissatisfied with election arrangements in 1865, he was extremely active in the process in 1868–1869. His main proposal in 1868, however, called for popular election of the president, an idea that obviously was not borrowed from the British. Rather, it could be said that Cerna's actual election by the chamber resembled Great Britain's indirect election of its prime minister.[24] Subsequently, García Granados's parliamentary opposition to Cerna adopted British patterns.

In a regime such as Cerna's, which tried to modernize while keeping in place the equipment of intellectual suffocation that had characterized Carrera's rule, Miguel García Granados was distinctly restless. He called for a policy that would be not only gradualist, like Cerna's, but also nonclerical in orientation. It also would be both parliamentary and popular in character, allowing for easy consideration of new ideas. Defeated politically and eventually persecuted, García Granados would be at last totally alienated from the regime. But by 1870 it appears that a significant element among the merchants of Guatemala City and most of the landed proprietors of the dynamic coffee industry felt much as he did. For these parties it would be Mexican events — specifically the triumph of Juárez's liberal reform — and not the security of familiar institutions inherited from Spain that indicated the wave of the future.

Domestic social processes, however, especially in regard to land tenure, probably weighed most heavily in the opposition to Cerna that had developed by 1870. The rural peasantry in Guatemala, including the village Indians reputed to be so long quiescent under Carrera, had in fact dissented strongly long before the caudillo's death in 1865. It is well documented that from the early 1850s on the coffee revolution had unleashed massive encroachments on village lands, which in turn stimulated a defensive backlash from the municipalities. It is also documented that in large measure both Carrera and Cerna turned a deaf ear to village complaints, both having committed themselves to developing the coffee culture. The basic technique for assault on Indian lands in the 1850s and 1860s, as described by J. C. Cambranes, fits the term "emphyteusis," defined in legal literature as a perpetual land-lease arrangement that allows the lessee to sublease and possibly to pass the lease on to his heirs. Cambranes stated:

> The Conservative Government permitted agrarian redistribution in Guatemala by fostering the handing over of land to private parties, which by law belonged to the peasant communities. . . . A key and characteristic contradiction in the agrarian redistribution plan promoted by the Conservatives, was that land leased to life tenants by the communities did not become the private property

of the parties who took possession of it. They did, however, retain the right to bequeath the land to their offspring, sublet it, even sell their acquired right to use and enjoy the fruits of it, but the land continued to be the legal property of the municipalities which had leased them in return for a negligible annual tax. In this way, a large percentage of finqueros, some of whom came to be prominent coffee growers, were simple tenant farmers on communal property during the Conservative period.[25]

There is no evidence of connections between García Granados and insurrectionists such as the Cruz family before 1870. His appears to have been strictly a parliamentary effort at change in the 1860s. Soon after his failure in the effort to reform presidential elections, one was held in the chamber on January 17, 1869. Cerna triumphed, but opposition continued to be significant, as indicated by the vote: Cerna 31, José Víctor Zavala 21, Luís Molina 3, Pedro de Aycinena 1, Manuel Echeverría 1. Although there were fifty-seven electors, only fifty-six signed the Acta that certified the result, García Granados again refusing. The British minister in Guatemala, who was present in the gallery, reported those last five scattered votes as abstentions, which they may have been effectively.[26]

Cruz Again

Cerna was inaugurated for his second term on May 24, 1869, several weeks after Serapio Cruz, joined by Rufino Barrios, renewed guerrilla raids along the northern border. Cruz launched his first attack in mid-March, trying to seize commercial goods in the border town of Nentón. He was repulsed, and the government exulted that he had not gotten a single weapon in the raid thanks to the diligence of the local *comandante*, a longtime favorite of the regime, who had pursued the Cruz force with dispatch. The *Gaceta* concluded that "Don Serapio Cruz, pardoned in the month of March, 1867, was for some time in Salvador, Honduras and Nicaragua and afterward moved to Chiapas and has remained in Comitán attempting to organize the invasion of Guatemalan territory. He has done it at last, gravely violating the agreement by which he was furnished a pardon." Through April and May the raids by Cruz and Barrios continued to be carried out by bands of twenty-five to seventy-five men. All were reported defeated.[27]

By mid-May the threat's real seriousness was acknowledged; a state of emergency was declared, and civil rights were suspended in response to the rebels' reported "deception and seduction" of Indians by promises of land distribution. Specifically suspended were guarantees in Articles 9, 15, and 18 through 24 of constitutional decree No. 62 of October 30, 1851, and Section 2 of the law of December 5, 1839. A second decree held anyone associated with Cruz responsible for the destruction caused by his raids. Yet another decree on May 10 required travelers in Los Altos and some parts of the mountainous northwestern part of the country to carry domestic or internal passports. Evidently this measure, which amounted to requiring identity cards, was aimed at whites and ladinos, because Indians and porters (*mozos de carga*) were specifically exempted from it.[28]

By May 1869 the *Gaceta* was, in effect, talking to itself about the Cruz threat. Its theme, not stated fully in one place but repeatedly alluded to, was that Serapio Cruz the ladino was seducing the Indians by exploiting their fear of ladinos. The usually unstated subtext was that Cruz — and any white or ladino who collaborated with him in this enterprise — was playing with the fire of racial war. Two years earlier, during the 1867 Cruz revolt, this idea of an isolated elite that must be cautious if it intended to survive had been stated clearly: A few hundred educated men in the towns could not really expect to have identical interests with many thousands of rural Indians and mestizos whose cultural experience remained distinctly non-European.[29]

In 1869 the theme was reinforced by bulletins that dealt with the Cruz gang's subversion of Indians in the villages. At Xeramux on April 27, according to the *Gaceta*, "a detachment of fifteen men from Huehuetenango commanded by Lt. Feliciano Abelar was led by the Indians through the rough terrain of the montaña to the point where an armed group of Cruz waited." Abelar's group was ambushed, and he apparently killed. He had been overconfident. Five members of the patrol made it back to town while Cruz passed through Nebaj, Chiantla, Huehuetenango, and Momostenango unscathed. The local corregidor's forces were divided, and he could not stop them. At Momostenango Cruz had about five hundred Indians and a few ladinos. About a hundred of his men were armed with shotguns and rifles, and others had machetes and knives, but most were unarmed. "It is said that in order to arouse and seduce the ignorant Indians [Cruz] invokes the name of General Carrera, whom he is supposed to represent," the *Gaceta* reported, adding that forces from Guatemala City had been sent to pursue the deluded group. "It is easy to comprehend the danger of the seduction that Cruz attempts to exercise and has begun to put into practice over a class whose tendencies and worries against the ladino class are well known. The abuse that is made of those fatal tendencies and of the ignorance of the Indians is lamentable, exposing the country to a war of castes in order to satisfy personal ambitions, whose results cannot be concealed from anyone."[30]

Government bulletins indicated that Cruz found it easier to arouse the Indians than to redirect their energies from their hatreds to his own purposes. After he left Huehuetenango, a force of between two hundred and three hundred Indians returned and attacked the aguardiente works, destroying the tools and machinery and making off with the bulk sugar stored there. Pursued by various local authorities, Cruz managed to stay ahead of them. Still, he had his problems. It was reported that "in Momostenango Cruz attempted to lead his force over the heights of Sija; but the Indians refused to accompany him and demanded to return to Nebaj and Ahuacatán and wait there for the ladinos in order to kill them."[31]

The government's frustration seemed to mirror the guerrilla warfare. It reported its border forces involved in sweeps of up to a thousand men trying to give protection to peaceful villages, prevent their subversion, and "punish severely disturbers of the peace." Commenting on broadsides of Cruz that had been transmitted to Guatemala City from the field, the government gave full rein to wishful thinking: Cruz was trying to deceive the unwary through airy promises of liberty and progress. This standard revolutionary tactic would not work because Guatemalans knew that the tyranny Cruz charged did not exist "and that those exercising authority are doing it with honor and with security and guarantees to all peaceful men." Citizens knew the hollowness of the words "liberty" and "progress" in Cruz's mouth and realized that only peace would bring them "security, welfare and improvement."[32]

President Cerna sought historical perspective on the matter in his second inaugural address on May 24, 1869. Reviewing his public career since its beginning in 1847, he saw his administration as pursuing "true progress" and "true liberty" under a guarantee of law and order. Some had mistaken his government's "lenience and moderation" for timidity. Under the circumstances, he was starting his second term determined to protect peaceful men and pursuits. He thought the future of Guatemala to be bright "if petty and stupid passions did not obstruct it." A few days later, his resolve seemed manifest in the announcement that a lieutenant in temporary command of the San Marcos garrison had completely defeated "the insurrectionist Rufino Barrios," who had attempted again to invade from Soconusco. Government troops had been reinforced "by Indians from San Pedro who have cooperated with decisive enthusiasm defending the tranquillity of their department." With eighteen men killed, Barrios had returned to Mexico with the "few" who were left.[33]

Body counts became important elements of government bulletins. It was reported, for instance, that on May 20 the seditionists under Cruz were defeated decisively in the heights of Chibul by the local army commander, one Colonel Batlle. Enemy losses: twenty-four dead, eighteen prisoners, and quantities of arms and ammunition taken. Government forces reported three of their own wounded. The *Gaceta* noted, "Colonel Batlle considers that this defeat would make it impossible for Cruz to continue his reckless enterprise, making him lose any prestige that he might have among the unwary individuals whom he had been able to seduce. Despite this, Colonel Batlle proposed to take the most active measures necessary to complete pacification of those localities." On further examination of the battle site three days later, fourteen more dead were recovered, along with seventeen muzzle loaders and six lances.[34]

In the summer of 1869 the question of Mexican involvement in these raids preoccupied the government. In early June it reviewed triumphantly the people's apparent indifference to Cruz's promises of cheap aguardiente and communal lands, speculating that in the future Mexican officials in Chiapas would be more helpful in preventing Cruz and Barrios from violating the frontier. By late July, however, government publications recognized that Mexican officials had done nothing to hinder Cruz from organizing there nor from crossing the border at Chacalá on a raid into Verapaz to raise the Indians. Nevertheless, these activities were seen as pointless: "Adequate measures have been taken to pursue and undo those gangs, which, without true political objective tend only to promote disorder, recruiting *perversos*, who are not lacking in any town, and attempting to awaken the worst instincts of many of the Indians against the ladino race."[35]

The Mexicans were considered feckless in regard to Guatemalan circumstances and preoccupied with their own problems in Chiapas, the details of which might make educated Guatemalans think twice. The indigenes of Chamula, Chiapas, said the *Gaceta*, had started a "horrifying war of the castes. . . . The barbarians made it clear . . . that their intent was hostile, even criminal; they began the war of castes of course with the death [of three leaders] and four more citizens of the so-called ladino class." A relief force sent by the Mexican government to re-establish order had to deal with a "mob of six or seven hundred indigenes" marching on the state capital, San Cristóbal.[36]

Through August, border raids and the tactics used to thwart them occupied the attention of government writers. The strain of trying always to present such disturbances as no threat to the government but indeed as a danger to the nation began to show: "While it is satisfying for a public writer to occupy himself with the interests of the nation . . . and to consecrate his attention to the promotion . . . of the arts of peace, free of the embarrassments that the machinations of ubiquitous discontents pro-duce; it is very hard for him to tell of events that, while far from indicating anarchy and retrocession, do indicate a situation not entirely exempt from worry." The sins of Serapio Cruz were then reviewed at pejorative length. The summer ended with the announcement that because a May decree, which required all who had been misled by Serapio Cruz to surrender and to give information had not been well circulated, provincial officers were to extend the deadline for compliance. Thereafter, punishment would be meted out to those who still would not cooperate.[37]

Crisis

The moment of political confrontation came in late autumn, when the Chamber of Deputies opened for a supposedly procedural session to keep the machinery of government functioning. This must have been García Granados's finest hour as parliamentary tribune in a country not much given to articulate public opposition. He moved boldly to end the execu-tive's state of emergency by promoting what amounted to a vote of no confidence. Two proposals were involved: that the government's decree of the previous May, declaring a state of siege, should be voided; and that the chamber should assume conduct of the war. The motion was easily defeated, but debate over it made clear the opposition's views. The gallery was packed daily, and the government was in a state of uneasy suspense until the assembly could be dismissed and public criticism again silenced. García Granados possessed a terse, biting style of speech, distinct from the mellif-luous oratory then customary to Guatemalan politicians. Apparently he pulverized opponents in the assembly with spare fact and logic, quite impersonally, saving his Spanish grace for the salon and social gatherings, where he and his wife captivated a generation of university students.[38]

A series of dispatches from the British chargé in Guatemala City in the autumn of 1869 foretold the coming crisis and provided the clearest available picture of Guatemala on the eve of the final struggle that led to revolution. The chargé, Edwin Corbett, strove to make the situation clear to his government in London. He saw Cruz's ability to defy the government with his extended guerrilla warfare to be based on strong support from the Indian population, although Corbett maintained that Cruz was "not a man of military or intellectual capacity." Beyond that, Cruz's harassing raids were seen to be motivated by personal ill-will against the government rather than by political philosophy. Many Guatemalans who were dissatisfied with the government saw Cruz as a crude but available instrument with which to bring down "the present personal and reactionary system of Government which has prevailed here for thirty years."

Corbett observed the widespread unpopularity of the government "except among those directly dependent upon it, or who are personally interested in upholding an antiquated system." He saw Cerna's system as totally alien to republican principles or to the "spirit" of the nineteenth century, noting, "The chief support of the present ruling party is to be found in the Church, and especially the Jesuits." The great influence of the latter on the Indian population and on the entire education system of the country, described by Corbett as of the most narrow and inefficient character, was a fact viewed with distaste by the "educated classes."

> The Liberal party on the occasion of the late reelection of the President Cerna . . . were defeated, and from the manner of the elections by the Chamber and certain high functionaries of the State it could not have been otherwise. The majority of the Chamber may be said, from the manner in which the elections are conducted and the irregularity of proceedings connected with them, to be nominees of the Government. . . . Thus it is hopeless to expect any change as long as the existing Constitution remains in force — though, if its provisions were faithfully carried out, the result might be different, but there is little prospect of the present Government altering their mode of proceeding in this direction, as it would be fatal to their tenure of office.[39]

Because it saw the situation this way, the Liberal Party, "which counts many men of capacity and fortune among its members," believed that the government could be changed only by revolution. The government took the public position that the liberal opposition was motivated completely by selfishness and personal desires for power. Corbett believed, however, that many of the liberals were sincere in their desire to improve their country by giving it more modern institutions and to develop its remarkable resources through liberal policies.

Corbett was writing in October 1869, when all seemed quiet in Guatemala, but he sensed that "some anxiety is felt at the future, as the general opinion is that sooner or later either through Cruz or some other means, a revolution is inevitable." He noted the government's determination to crush the insurrection by sending three thousand men to insurgent areas.

It was common knowledge, however, that the soldiers were not entirely dependable and that their conduct toward the population was very bad: "They rob and ill-use in every way the unfortunate Indians and thus naturally indispose them against the Government and induce them to favor, as far as they can, the insurrection, commanded by a leader of their own origin who treats them well."

Thus Corbett found the country in a critical state. He thought if the government succeeded in taking Cruz, a doubtful prospect, "the existing system may continue some time longer, but meanwhile the present state of disquiet and apprehension is very prejudicial to all kinds of business." The cost to the treasury of maintaining so many soldiers in the field hurt the economy because agriculture, the "only" resource of the country, lost the many laborers forced into the army. Depredation of harvest and property was great on both sides, because their natural defenders were forced to be absent.[40]

Corbett noted that social pressure for political change was growing in another way. In response to a British Foreign Office circular seeking information on the cost of living of the diplomatic corps in various countries, he reported routinely on Guatemala City. The circular requested and Corbett provided a comparison of the cost of living in 1850 with that of the current year (1869). Figures for the earlier year reflected the economy before the battle of La Arada (1851), the usual reference point for Carrera's stabilization of the country. His comparison is thus useful as a gauge of the consequences to the consumer of economic development under Carrera and Cerna. "House rent is now generally double, and in many cases treble, what it was in 1850," he said. He himself had "the greatest difficulty in finding a suitable house" when he arrived in Guatemala in the mid-1860s, having finally to pay £300 a year (about $100 per month) for one that would not have been large enough had he brought his entire family. The price of furniture had gone up by half, mainly because it was of better quality than in 1850. "Carriages are mostly imported from the United States, England, or Germany, a few only being built in the country; they are much more numerous than in 1850; the cost of the keep of horses has doubled since that date." The coming of the coffee culture brought many foreigners and had driven up the wages of domestic servants significantly. "The general style of living is certainly more expensive now than it was in 1850. The price of beef has remained nearly stationary, that of mutton, for which there is a greater demand now than formerly, has increased 50 percent since 1850; the price of vegetables has risen in about the same proportion in the same period, and the other necessaries of life from 25 to 50 percent."[41]

Ten days before the Chamber of Representatives reconvened, Corbett noted that the country's political crisis was deepening because of the government's inability to defeat or even to contain Cruz. He considered reliable information regarding Cruz's force to be scarce but believed that the best private estimate was five hundred ladinos well armed and orga- nized, two hundred Indians poorly armed and "without discipline." What seemed clear was that for four or five months Cruz had dominated a significant part of the country and that government forces, under inade- quate field commanders, had proven to be ineffective. Corbett thought Cruz was now stronger than ever and that the size of his army was limited only by his ability to arm and feed it.

Cruz was extremely popular among the Indian population and had "abstained scrupulously" from injury to private property, except for univer- sal pillage of the stores of the aguardiente monopoly. Popular resentment against that form of taxation and desire to drink the supplies guaranteed that result. "Cruz appears to be well informed of all the movements of the Troops sent against him; on the other hand the Leaders of the latter know nothing of his movements and he appears to be able to move about in all directions through an extensive district of the country with the utmost impunity."[42]

It appeared to Corbett that the government was trying to conceal the seriousness and expense of the situation by underestimating not only the size and strength of Cruz's forces but also the size of the army sent against the insurgents. Although the government claimed its force to be no more than nine hundred, common knowledge indicated it could not be less than two thousand and probably was more. Morale in the army, of both officers and men, appeared to be increasingly shaky. The desire for "a more liberal system . . . one more in accordance with the progressive ideas of the time," was now focusing on Cruz as a rallying point for discontent. President Cerna was so concerned that he considered taking command of the field forces himself, but it seemed possible that if he did, Guatemala City would rise in revolt while he was away.

> The President is very unpopular — except in the part of the country to which he belongs and where he held for some years the post of Corregidor — not on account of any acts or proceeding attributed to him, but he is despised as a political nonentity — ruled entirely by the Minister Aycinena, and as a man totally without initiative or will of his own. He is an excellent man in private life, and a very rigid Catholic — a prolific source of the contempt felt

for him by a large section of the public who attribute the state of
the country to the influence of the Priests.[43]

The raids of Cruz and his confederates continued through November
and early December with growing success, which caused the government
not only to dismiss the chamber sine die but also to reprimand the
parliamentary opposition. The *Gaceta* commented that scenes of desolation
caused by Cruz's recent raids were beginning to look like those of 1848, also
caused by Cruz. "This ought to capture the serious attention of all honorable
and intelligent men, who cannot see with indifference the subversion of
public order with the sole object of satisfying the ambition of an individual
and of the few criminals or beguiled who accompany him on his enterprise,"
the *Gaceta* urged. Accompanying reports indicate a condition of classical
guerrilla warfare. Indeed, Cruz's growing success, both military and political, received no check or hindrance until December 10, when he attacked
Huehuetenango with his main force and was repulsed with a loss of more
than one hundred men and several of his officers, including his son,
Ramón.[44]

A subsequent report of the burial of Ramón Cruz included information
that a government surgeon captured by the insurgents had been forced to
treat the wounds of Rufino Barrios, three bullet holes in the arm. It was also
claimed that the number of insurgent wounded had risen to 250. This clear
defeat at Huehuetenango, however tactical it might be, did help the
government and its army to regroup psychologically during the ensuing six
weeks. When Cruz issued a circular blaming destruction of part of the town
on its defenders because they had refused to fight in "open country," the
government rejoined that the battle would go down in history as a crime
premeditated by Cruz. One church (del Calvario) had been burned, another (the parish church) attacked. Thus, the people could know what to
expect "from those hordes whom their gangleader continues calling an
army of liberation!"[45]

A masterstroke by the government ended the insurgency of Serapio
Cruz on January 23, 1870. Cerna had received information on the previous
day that the forces of Cruz were passing east of the capital toward the
mountains. By nightfall the reports were confirmed, and about 9:30 P.M.
his close associate, the veteran general Antonino Solares, was dispatched
eastward from the capital with four hundred men of the Santa Rosa
battalion. By forced march through the night, he located the enemy not
far from the large hacienda of Palencia. Keeping his troops out of sight,
Solares followed Cruz's column to Palencia with the object of achieving

surprise. Cruz entered the hacienda patio about 6 A.M., upbraiding those in charge and threatening to shoot them. Some of his troops foraged for food in the surrounding farm buildings while the others remained in the central patio.

Solares, approaching cautiously from the east, divided his force into small bands and surrounded the village complex still unperceived. He commanded personally the company that opened fire on the central patio. The rebels took cover behind a stone wall encircling the central buildings and despite their surprise resisted the vigorous attack of government troops. Cruz mounted quickly and joined in the bitter combat, which was hand to hand at many points. Solares was wounded in the foot and had to cut down one guerrilla attacker with his saber. After being dislodged, the rebels fought in the open only briefly before fleeing in all directions, closely pursued. Cruz, recognized and pursued by Solares, rode out by the cemetery but was thrown into a small, treacherous ravine nearby — indeed, Solares almost fell in himself. There, his leg broken in the fall, Cruz was killed by two enlisted men, though he defended himself fiercely (*con furor*) to the end.[46]

Immediate pursuit of the scattering guerrillas was effective. Many were killed and many wounded and captured, and more than one hundred weapons were taken, along with several boxes of powder and more than forty pack animals. However, the real accomplishment of this event — which would be called for the rest of the Cerna period *el hecho de armas de Palencia* — was the confirmed death of Serapio Cruz. The proof was dramatically exhibited that same afternoon when a special courier, sent from Palencia on horseback, rode through the streets of the capital displaying the severed head of Cruz. Two days later Solares and his army, after mopping up and resting at Palencia, reached Guatemala City and were greeted on the outskirts by President Cerna and an entourage of notables.

Gen. Antonino Solares had been a fixture in the conservative regime for thirty years. His service with Carrera had begun in the guerrilla phase before 1840, and he had been a close comrade-in-arms of Cerna since at least 1847. During most of his career, Solares had served in the eastern provinces, far from the political center. But in the conservative view, this modest ladino gained immortality at Palencia. Riding through the cheering crowds in the streets of the capital that afternoon in late January 1870, Solares began to receive his due. It was remarked that he had not even visited the capital for many years until his recent assignment against Cruz, "coming now providentially to give in a few hours perhaps the most important service of his thirty-year career."

He received the Central American equivalent of a Roman triumph. His troops, "who loved him more as a father than as a chief," gave him an ovation in the patio of the government palace as the president announced that Antonino Solares had been raised to the rank of field marshal. The government obituary of Serapio Cruz achieved an almost baroque contrast in its views of the two men who had contended at Palencia. "Trying to slip into the eastern mountains," it read, "Cruz came in search of death; there in an hour and a half the iniquitous work he had laboriously prepared through several years was destroyed. A general in the service of the government, more rewarded than he merited; a rebel caught and pardoned, faithless to his oath and word of honor; a leader of arsonists and assassins, Cruz was led by Providence to the place where he had to expiate his sins." The editor summed up Cruz's career as one of those "terrible lessons of history, which teach that passions and blindness lead to the abyss," concluding that peace would now inevitably be re-established and that the republic would continue "on its march of progress and reforms."[47] In contrast to Cruz, Solares had achieved patriotic immortality: "Field Marshal Don Antonino Solares has returned with the Santa Rosa unit to its post where he serves the State with fidelity and modesty, carrying with him the satisfaction of having fulfilled perfectly his duty and the well-wishes of a grateful people."[48]

A major crisis had been resolved, but the government had now to decide how it would capitalize on its victory. Essentially, three political options were available. It could try to rule as before, in a virtually despotic manner but allowing debate in the chamber to resume. It could change the constitution and give the opposition a real chance to compete on the theory that peace was more important than party, that tension would be reduced, problems would be resolved, and revolution would be averted in the future. Or it could choose thorough despotism, repressing all dissent. In late February 1870 it chose the last course — and Guatemala entered the vortex of revolution.

Notes

1. Ministerio de hacienda, Acuerdo sobre remate de estancos de aguardiente y chicha, para los años de 1866 y 1867 . . . , *Gaceta* XIV, 88 (September 15, 1865), 4.

2. "Estancos de aguardiente y chicha," *Gaceta* XV, 23 (August 8, 1865), 184–185.

3. Estatutos de la compañía de aguardientes de Guatemala, *Gaceta* XV, 28 (October 9, 1866), 221–223, also at 185; Vicente de la Hoz to editor, *Gaceta* XV, 25 (September 1866), 200.

4. Vicente Cerna, Mensage . . . a la cámara de representantes en la apertura de sus cuartas sesiones del tercer período constitucional, *Gaceta* XV, 32 (December 5, 1866), 253–255.

5. Estatutos de la compañía de aguardientes de Guatemala, *Gaceta* XV, 54 (August 6, 1867), 429–431. N. B., Anuncios, Compañía de aguardientes de Guatemala, Remite de los estancos de chicha, para el ano de 1870, *Gaceta* XVI, 40 (November 4, 1870), 2. These are later arrangements that appear similar to those in force before the company was organized.

6. "Comisión del gobierno en Santa Catarina," *Gaceta* XIV, 89 (September 24, 1865), 3. N. B. David McCreery, "State Power, Indigenous Communities, and Land in Nineteenth-Century Guatemala, 1820–1920," in Carol A. Smith, ed., *Guatemalan Indians and the State* (Austin: University of Texas Press, 1990), 103–104. McCreery describes the inhabitants of Santa Catarina Ixtahuacán as being "notoriously ferocious" in the almost universal village land disputes of the late nineteenth century. His extensive archival research reveals that officials ordinarily gave the village a wide berth and did not really understand what was happening in it.

7. *Ibid.*; Comunicación del Sr. Magistrado D. José María Saravia, dando cuenta al gobierno de su comisión en el pueblo Santa María Ixtahuacán, *Gaceta* XIV, 89 (September 24, 1865), 2.

8. Cf. "Tranquilidad pública," *Gaceta* XV, 14 (May 9, 1866), 109, and "Puerto de San José," 21 (July 14, 1866), 168; Decretos sobre la sedición promovida por Don Serapio Cruz, *Gaceta* XV, 37 (February 7, 1867), 293–294.

9. "Tranquilidad pública," *Gaceta* XV, 37 (February 7, 1867), 295.

10. Boletín de noticias, 1, 13 de febrero de 1867, *Gaceta* XV, 38 (February 16, 1867), 302–303.

11. "Tranquilidad pública," *Gaceta* XV, 40 (March 9, 1867), 320–321.

12. Acuerdo que se dispone de los comprendidos en la sedición de D. Serapio Cruz, 16 de marzo de 1867, *Gaceta* XV, 41 (March 21, 1867), 327.

13. "Exmo. Sr. Presidente," *Gaceta* XV, 43 (April 16, 1867), 341.

14. "Frontera de Chiapas," *Gaceta* XV, 45 (May 11, 1867), 363–364.

15. Boletín de noticias, 16 de agosto de 1867, *Gaceta* XV, 56 (August 23, 1867), 446–447.

16. Vicente Cerna, Mensaje, dirijido . . . a la Cámara de Representantes . . . 25 de noviembre de 1867, *Gaceta* XV, 64 (December 7, 1867), 509–511.

17. "Fin del año," *Gaceta* XV, 66 (January 3, 1868), 526.

18. Boletín de noticias, 29 de abril de 1868, *Gaceta* XV, 75 (May 1, 1868), 599–600.

19. Acta de la sesión de la asamblea general el día 3 de mayo de 1865, *Gaceta* XIV, 72 (May 8, 1868).

20. J. Antonio Villacorta, *Historia de la república de Guatemala (1821–1921)* (Guatemala: Tipografía Nacional, 1960), 155–156, 158–160.

21. Miguel García Granados, *Memorias del General Miguel García Granados*, 3rd ed., vol. 1 (Guatemala: Ministerio de Educación Pública, 1952, [1877, 1896]), 17–18.

22. Ramón Salazar, *Tiempo viejo, recuerdos de mi juventud*, 2nd ed. (Guatemala: Ministerio de Educación Pública, 1957, [1896]), 142–143. Clemente Marroquín Rojas, journalist, historian, and vice president of Guatemala (1966–1970), in an interview with Wayne M. Clegern (Guatemala City, July 1971), referred to García Granados's leadership of the "ala izquierda" of the conservatives.

23. García Granados, *Memorias*, vol. 4, 424–427.

24. Cámara de representantes, sesión de . . . 2a de diciembre de 1868, *Gaceta* XVI, 6 (February 25, 1869), 1; sesión de . . . 30 de diciembre de 1868, 7 (March 2, 1869), 1–2; sesión de . . . 5 de enero [and] sesión de . . . 7 de enero de 1869, 8 (March 10, 1869), 1–2.

25. J. Castellanos Cambranes, *Coffee and Peasants: The Origins of the Modern Plantation Economy in Guatemala, 1853–1897*, Clara Clason Höök, trans. and ed. (Stockholm: SAREC, 1985), 84–85, 88–89.

26. Cámara de representantes, elección de presidente de la república, *Gaceta* XVI, 2 (January 22, 1869), reported that García Granados "departed before the signing"; Edwin Corbett (British chargé in Guatemala) to Lord Stanley, No. 5, Guatemala, January 17, 1869, FO 15/139, 19–20.

27. "Frontera de Chiapas," *Gaceta* XVI, 10 (March 24, 1869), 6; "Frontera de Chiapas," 13 (April 16, 1869), 5; "Frontera de Chiapas," 14 (April 27, 1869), 4.

28. Ministerio de gobernación, Decretos (two dated May 8, 1869), *Gaceta* XVI, 16 (May 12, 1869), 1. Another, dated May 10, 1869, required internal passports.

29. Editorial, *La semana* I, 100 (January 13, 1867), 1.

30. Boletín de noticias 1, 7 de mayo de 1869, *Gaceta* XVI, 16 (May 12, 1869), 2.

31. Boletín de noticias 2, 10 mayo 1869, *Gaceta* XVI, 17 (May 12, 1869), 2–3.

32. Boletín de noticias 3, 13 de mayo de 1869, *Gaceta* XVI, 17 (May 22, 1869), 2.

33. Vicente Cerna, Mensage [inaugural], 24 de mayo de 1869, *Gaceta* XVI, 18 (May 31, 1869); Boletín de noticias 4, 28 de mayo de 1869, 18 (May 31, 1869), 2.

34. Boletín de noticias 5, 25 mayo 1869, and 6, 28 de mayo de 1869, *Gaceta* XVI, 18 (May 31, 1869), 2.

35. Boletín de noticias 8, 21 de julio de 1869, *Gaceta* XVI, 26 (July 27, 1869), 1–2.

36. "Chiapas, la guerra de castas," *Gaceta* XVI, 26 (July 27, 1869), 2–3.

37. "Situación," *Gaceta* XVI, 27 (August 2, 1869), 2; Ministerio de gobernación, Acuerdo, 30 de agosto de 1869, 31 (August 31, 1869), 1.

38. Edwin Corbett to Lord Clarendon, No. 77, Guatemala, November 27, 1869, FO 15/140, 96–98; Corbett to Clarendon, No. 81, Guatemala, December 12, 1869, 161–168; and Rámon Salazar, *Tiempo viejo*, 141, 148–151.

39. Corbett to Clarendon, No. 69, Guatemala, October 14, 1869, FO 15/140, 44–45.

40. *Ibid.*

41. Corbett to Clarendon, No. 75, Guatemala, November 11, 1869, FO 15/140, 80–87.

42. Corbett to Clarendon, No. 76, Guatemala, November 15, 1869, FO 15/140, 88–95.

43. *Ibid.*

44. Boletín de noticias 12, *Gaceta* XVI, 44 (November 30, 1869), 2; Corbett to Clarendon, No. 81, Guatemala, December 12, 1869, FO 15/140, 161–168. See also Boletín de noticias 13, 7 de diciembre de 1869, *Gaceta* XVI, 45 (December 8, 1869); 14, 12 de diciembre de 1869; and 16, 14 de diciembre de 1869, 46 (December 16, 1869).

45. Boletín de noticias 16, 14 de diciembre 1869, *Gaceta* XVI, 46 (December 16, 1869); 17, 20 de diciembre de 1869, 47 (December 22, 1869), 4.

46. Boletín de noticias 20, 26 de enero 1870, *Gaceta* XVI, 52 (January 28, 1870), 3; FO 15/147, Corbett to Clarendon, No. 5, Guatemala, January 31, 1870, 67–73.

47. *Ibid; Gaceta* XVI, 52 (January 28, 1870), 4.

48. *Ibid.*; cf. Vicente Cerna, Presidente de la república al ejército, 28 de enero de 1870, *Gaceta* XVI, 53 (February 5, 1870), 1.

4
The Vortex, 1870–1871

The death of Serapio Cruz in January 1870 did not bring an end to the state of siege declared eight months earlier. Instead, the Cerna government proceeded with a policy of repression as a means to progress. The year 1870 featured vigorous pursuit of difficult reforms, and the government claimed partisan debate would hamper such efforts. Information captured in the last days of Cruz convinced the government that treasonous designs lurked in the opposition. Within the week, José María Samayoa and Manuel Larrave, dissenting members of the elite, were arrested on suspicion and thrown into the dungeons of nearby Fort San José. The local diplomatic corps considered their arrests a disgrace and incarceration in the dungeons uncivilized. Diplomatic intervention — and bail payments in the amount of $20,000 for Samayoa and $10,000 for Larrave — quickly relieved their plight. They were sent into exile and forbidden to return without governmental permission. In the same crackdown, an order went out for the arrest of Miguel García Granados.[1]

Repression

Banishment of three prominent members of the opposition in this fashion may have been illegal, but the government wished to eliminate their attacks in the chamber. García Granados eluded government arrest by seeking sanctuary in the home of Field Marshal José Víctor Zavala, his first cousin and close associate. Zavala, runner-up in the last presidential election and an exceedingly popular public figure, could not be bullied by the government, but his power was limited. The pressure on Zavala was such that two weeks seemed the longest he could provide shelter. Upon learning of orders to take García Granados from his domicile by force, Zavala asked the British chargé, Edwin Corbett, to afford García Granados sanctuary in the British legation until his exile could be negotiated. Corbett reluctantly agreed, and García Granados was spirited into the compound — soon surrounded by government troops — for ten days. Corbett stood fast against the government's demand that he should return the dissident. Terms similar to those granted the other two exiles were arranged, and García Granados, after paying a $10,000 bond, proceeded to the port of San José and took ship for Panama.[2]

The political intensity of the government in banishing García Granados was indicated by its published version of the circumstances, accompanied prominently by the information that Corbett was leaving soon for Europe. Corbett objected to such blatant linkage of his departure with the recent showdown. He addressed a note to Pedro de Aycinena, the minister of foreign affairs, pointing out that the leave had been requested the previous November and that his "imminent departure had nothing whatever to do with the incident which has occurred between the Government and this Legation." Corbett insisted that his clarification receive publicity equal to that given the preceding report. He explained to his superior in London that this exercise was necessary because of "the jesuitical character of this Government," which, he thought, had tried to extract spurious political advantage from his going on leave.[3] Efforts to pursue a forceful policy of development did require a certain prestige to enhance official authority, and the British legation's defiance in the sanctuary incident clearly tended toward the opposite effect — hence the government's desire to imply publicly that it had gained some kind of satisfaction from the affair. With the same objective Cerna made a well-publicized display of largesse to victims on both sides of the recent rebellion.[4]

When the Chamber of Deputies reconvened on April 4, 1870, Cerna's message was unusually long. He cited the order and tranquility re-established by "the brilliant feat of arms of Palencia." He also expressed appreciation for the loyalty and contributions of everyone in the country and city who had supported order and authority firmly against the "few who had tried to substitute their capricious will for that of the majority of the citizenry." He offered a personal defense of the current policy of repression: Though it was well known that he disliked authoritarian measures, the needs of society now required them. The chamber had witnessed his forbearance toward political provocation, but one could not forbear in the face of sedition. The blame for the extraordinary powers currently invested in the executive lay squarely on those guilty individuals who since the death of Carrera had not hesitated to seek for Guatemala "the evils that afflict and annihilate other unfortunate sections of Spanish America."[5]

This proclamation was buttressed by articles reprinted in the *Gaceta* invoking both papal authority and Central American backwardness to justify a controlled press. A week after Cerna's message appeared in the *Gaceta*, an article from a Catholic journal in Rome, *Eco di Roma*, was published in the same pages clarifying the papal view of the press in relation to the Vatican Council then under way.

> Due to circumstances, Prudence requires [the Vatican] to prescribe for all acts of the Council the law of secrecy which has had to be imposed only once in earlier Councils. This precaution seems more necessary than ever in an epoch in which a powerful impiety seeks all occasions for exciting hatred against the Catholic Church and its doctrine. Consequently we prohibit each and every one of the fathers or of the officials of the Council, the theologians, the canonists, and all who in any way aid the fathers or the officials of the Council, from divulging or saying anything at all, outside of the Council, about the decrees and propositions that may be made, as well as the discussions and opinions expressed. We ordain further that the officials of the Council who are not Bishops, and the others who having received from Us a special charge, have to attend the deliberations of the Council in order to discharge their office, give oath of fulfilling faithfully their duties, and of keeping the faith in secrecy of everything which happens in connection with the particular duties with which they are charged.

The editor of *Eco di Roma* said this papal view explained why his journal felt bound to secrecy even though it did not attend the council: "We . . . believe we are required not to know and not to wish to know of the interior life . . . of the sacred assembly but rather that which effectively and by authorization is official [and thus] pertains to the public domain." This procedure was both just and convenient for *Eco*'s readers because it would guarantee them purity in doctrine, exactitude in narration, and rectitude in judgment. Speculators or mercenaries, through venality and malice, would invent presumptuous and untrue accounts of the council. "But, thanks be to God, we are Catholics, who do not elude the fulfillment of our duty by cunning distinctions." There was ample cause to tell the reader what was important to him: "In Rome that is completely free which is worthy of being called entirely good; and that which is not entirely good ought not to be free in Rome nor in other places."[6]

Reprinted in Guatemala, the *Eco di Roma* article helped to establish
not just a pious atmosphere but also a convenient frame of reference. Such
an iron-clad defense of repression of thought made Cerna's appear mild by
comparison. In the following month the *Gaceta* ran an article published
under the Dueñas regime in El Salvador that applied the notion of self-re-
straint explicitly to Central American journalism. The writer focused on
the importance of journalism and the obstacles facing a public writer in
Central America, but first he wallowed in the idea of progress:

> The human species obeys the law of progress, which . . . is
> nothing else than the rationalized desire to improve one's condi-
> tion. . . . Happiness, insofar as it is attainable amid the meanness
> and miseries of life, is the ideal that man pursues across the earth.
> . . . We do not rest in the fight to supply ourselves the fullest measure
> of wellbeing that we can obtain. Forward, always forward! is the
> device of man! The astonishing prosperity of nations which had
> remained for some centuries in the most complete backwardness,
> teaches us that only with work is a desirable future attained.
> Humanity marches ceaselessly then, in pursuit of progress and uses
> all means available to attain it.

He held journalism to be an advanced sentinel of order, liberty, and
improvement in any country where it fulfilled its civilizing mission. The
press could sell out in various ways, including the pursuit of vulgarity,
although properly it should inform the public about useful branches of
knowledge and support government efforts to enlighten citizens. But, the
writer added, "the endeavor to conserve general tranquillity and to embed
in the spirit of citizens ideas of order and habits of hard work is, without
any doubt, the most imperious obligation of the conscientious and enlightened journalist." This task was difficult because everywhere, and especially
in Central America, public writers were the target of venomous criticism
from troublemakers. It was impossible to satisfy everyone. The article
lamented, "Among us the press . . . still cannot be allowed the latitude
available today in some countries of Europe and in some sections of South
America, where, without discrediting the social order, social interests can
be discussed freely and the microscope of the most severe and even
passionate examination is applied to the political and administrative acts
of governments." Central America's history of civil wars and instability
made it impossible to expose the present peace and harmony to an abuse
of freedom of the press that might bring anarchy, retrocession, and discredit.
"Some day, later, when the present governments may have disappeared,

and their name and deeds remain no more than a memory of the country, justice will be done" to the freedoms all favor.[7]

This proposition to reduce freedom of the press by institutionalizing it was totally in character for Guatemala. The gradualism of the Cerna regime was so strong that distinctions between reform and development in its policies were difficult to discern. It used the term "corporation" to identify not private companies or enterprises but rather the traditional institutions, official and semiofficial, that largely ruled the country. These entities carried out the government's policies in great measure, whether the policies were standpat in character or geared for change. Typically, a single corporation carried out both kinds of policies and was itself viewed as an agent of progress. This view is reflected in an assessment of the value of annual reports of the corporations, seen to be "so many other workers for the general good: collaborators with the supreme government in the difficult task of impelling the country on the path of its improvement, they require the cooperation of all good citizens who are able in some manner to contribute to achievement of the objective of their institution." The press should do likewise, the *Gaceta* charged; "therefore we always receive with sympathy all that which relates to the march of the corporations."[8]

Development

The colonial system of landholding inherited from the Spanish needed revision in a state where agricultural land was the major capital resource. A functional expansion of export agriculture in Guatemala would require the elite to grasp firmly several new, interrelated ideas on law, business, and agriculture. A modern mortgage law would be needed, but it would furnish merely one plank in the platform for an economic takeoff. On August 1, 1870, the lead editorial of the Economic Society's journal dealt with the large problem of a modern economy, and a subordinate article argued specifically for repeal of the usury law. The editorialist saw Central American agriculture as divided into two basic branches: "1st. Agriculture proper, which furnishes us the daily bread, meat, milk that nourishes us and the vegetable and animal fibers that clothe us. 2nd. Industrial and mercantile agriculture that thanks to our geographical position and our privileged climate, extracts from the soil products of such value that the entire world buys them." The two types of agriculture must not be confused, he cautioned. Agriculture proper had been so neglected that Guatemala now used "degenerate" seeds and raised inferior livestock. As a result, the country had to import food it could have grown domestically and pay unreasonably high prices for poor meat products. It had been alleged that the great increase in cultivation of coffee and sugarcane caused the shortage of food commodities. In partial refutation of that charge, it was noted that the Indians who raised wheat could cultivate neither coffee nor cane, yet they could not fully supply the country with wheat because of population growth and a rise in the standard of living. Agricultural prosperity caused money to circulate in "areas where before it was unknown." Establishment of peace and better communication routes would keep pressure on the food supply.[9]

The companion article on usury repeal analyzed at length the problem of interest and credit in Guatemala, emphasizing also that the value of all material things is determined by supply and demand. The interest charged for money responded to the same law as did other commodities: "The true means of bringing down interest is to give guarantees to the lenders. When they know their capital is secure and that they will be paid their profits faithfully the price of money will be only for its *use* not for the *risk*. Thus the statutes should allow free play of the market." This point had to be made because the Guatemalan law of October 22, 1840, limited interest, fixing 6 percent as the maximum "and punishing the creditor who exceeds the limit with the loss of all recompense, even the legal ones." This law was originally intended to help the borrower, but now it hurt him by making capital unavailable. In summary, the article asserted, "the law of 1840 is bad for enterprisers and capitalists, and good for fraudulent debtors." A country such as Guatemala needed abundant, cheap capital, so "abolition of that law would produce, in our judgment, the best results for the national wealth."[10]

With some reservations, these arguments tended to advocate standard nineteenth-century laissez-faire economic policy, which meant that, as export agriculture grew, the problem of poverty would have to be rationalized. Such rationalization was offered in an article on Catholic society, expressing a conservative viewpoint that saw pauperism as a natural phenomenon. "Catholicism says: give food to the hungry; give drink to the thirsty; clothe the naked; redeem the captive. But if man does not work and save/economize/etc. where will he find the food for the hungry? In order to satisfy these necessities it is necessary to work or to steal, and the seventh commandment . . . has said: thou shalt not steal. Political economy has not created nor has it cured the leprosy of pauperism . . . an infirmity as natural in civilized societies as old age is in individuals."[11] The clear implication was that government reforms should be aimed at bolstering the economic mechanism, enabling the country to develop to the point that the successful could give appropriate aid to the poor.

Perhaps the best example of the connection between reform and development during the Cerna regime was the attempt to solve a severe currency problem and introduce simultaneously the decimal system. Not only did this reform reveal a pragmatic initiative to rectify an increasingly profound commercial and agricultural problem in Guatemalan life, it also demonstrated a desire to be a more modern nation capable of functioning in a first-class way in the world trading system. The solution even had a radical aspect — it was argued that it would cut through a superstructure of accumulated problems in Guatemalan society by means of a single, coordinated policy. The clear ideological implication was that, with minimal intervention in the economy, the reform would put the social machine back in balance and allow it to develop in a relatively free manner.

The Guatemalan economy, after decades of some disorientation, grew steadily in the 1860s, aided largely by the Panama railroad, the development of California, and the export of coffee. By 1868 the new prosperity brought a countervailing currency crisis described classically in the following terms: "In its monetary currency the Republic presently suffers from continuous, annoying and ruinous hindrances for its industry, which affect even the smallest and most frequent domestic transactions. This disagreeable and pernicious situation is inherited (*viene de atrás*), grows worse each day, and if a remedy is not found will become unbearable." Ninety percent of the currency in the country was silver, and 60 percent of the silver was damaged (*recortada* or *macuquina*); 20 percent of the currency consisted of well-minted Guatemalan coins, and 15 percent were old Spanish or Mexican coins or specimens of other origin too worn to be distinguishable. Only 4 percent of the currency was made up of European and North American coins in good condition.[12]

This crisis brought on the monetary-decimal reform of 1870, in which the youthful Enrique Palacios played a critical role. Palacios, well-educated son of the elite, devotee of the Church, and a conservative of renown since the assassination attempt on him in Nicaragua, was perhaps the most characteristic figure in the Cerna regime's efforts to modernize Guatemala. Although loyal to the old regime, with all clarity he wanted a vigorous future. Left with a shattered cheekbone by the assassin in 1865, Palacios had hovered between life and death for a few weeks in the residence of the Nicaraguan archbishop before being returned to Guatemala for convalescence.

As he recovered among friends and family in the autumn of 1865, Palacios was marked as a conservative martyr-hero and as a literary success. His book-length description and analysis of Guatemala, written in Nicaragua just before the assassination attempt, had been published in installments in *La semana* (April to July 1865). More than a century later it remains an impressive effort, and in 1865 it lent great stature to Palacios in Guatemala. His distinguished career, 1865–1870, is not to be wondered at: secretary to the council of state, 1866; vice director of the economic society, 1866; deputy in the legislative chamber, 1868; and special envoy to the United States and Europe "with various important commissions" for the entire year of 1869. After his return he was named councilor of state and superintendent of the mint.[13]

The monetary-decimal reform was Palacios's crowning effort in civil government, a triumph shared by the consensus within the Cerna regime. The monetary analysis of 1868, noted previously, concluded that the best solution would be to get a loan to carry out a number of needed projects, including demonetization of defective coinage and standardization of the currency. The objective, in other words, was to float a single, multifaceted monetary reform through an injection of money into the national economy. Thus, the most important of the commissions Palacios carried to Europe in 1869 was to negotiate a loan for £500,000. While he was gone, a presidential decree put in place the legal basis of a new currency, the metric decimal system, by declaring the metric equivalents to be used in new coinage.[14]

The Guatemalan government wished to standardize its currency in order to stay in step with those European and American countries (France, Italy, Belgium, Spain, Germany, Chile, Colombia, Ecuador, Peru, and Uruguay) that since 1865 had begun to unify their currencies on the basis of the metric-decimal system. The basic treaty of this monetary union, concluded in 1865, was an open one; any country could adhere to it by declaring itself bound by the treaty's principles. The resulting standard table of intrinsic values for the different currencies based on standard measures would aid foreign trade by providing easier convertibility.[15] By October 1870 the reform had been launched, the loan funds were in hand, the comprehensive monetary law of September 21, 1870, had been decreed, and the mint was ready to go to work. Official explanation of the reform now could be and had to be presented in the most persuasive terms to the Guatemalan elite, its declared beneficiaries and of necessity its practical executors. Accordingly, the full argument was delivered in the *Gaceta*: These arrangements had been made to solve the problems of Guatemala's monetary capital. Money was both a measuring device and an object of inherent worth; it was this double character that created its unique value as an instrument of exchange. The basic monetary unit in Guatemala, the peso, must conform to this basic condition. The principle was not so strictly applicable to fractional currency, or change (*moneda de ajuste*), which was more a measuring device and less important for its inherent value. The macuquina, or inferior coins (known variously as *plata cortada*, *plata recortada*, and *lisa redonda*), that predominated in Guatemala had lost much of their intrinsic value but still possessed their legal authority. Guatemalan pesos coined in three different epochs had been based on at least three different formulas of silver content and thus had different intrinsic values. And, of course, counterfeit money was circulating. All these factors reduced confidence in Guatemala's currency.

Although macuquina was legal tender in Guatemala, it was often refused in business transactions in favor of *quedanes* (commercial paper or IOUs), and it was impossible to ship abroad because the outside world would accept it only at its intrinsic value. Thus, the good coins were shipped abroad, and Gresham's law was fulfilled. In Central America alone, the indigo trade with El Salvador and the cattle trade with Honduras and Nicaragua caused an export of 400,000 to 600,000 pesos per year. Despite continuous production by the mint, it was impossible to keep good coinage in Guatemala. Macuquina dominated the national currency, hindering commercial, industrial, agricultural, and even domestic transactions. The public appeared to be unanimous in demanding elimination of macuquina and availability of correct currency. A single monetary standard was needed to solve this complex situation. Further, it was urged that this need to standardize, combined with the recall and demonetization of macuquina, made this the ideal time to introduce decimal reform, the wave of the future.[16]

Explanation of the reform was lengthy and cogent, taking into account every technical complication the government could imagine. In the end, however, the nature of its exhortation was an admission that willingness of the public to accept the reform was crucial to its success.

> The reform decreed is of high importance, it is an act of progress which does honor to the country, and is an improvement which can only be received with enthusiasm, unless one has an interest in continuing the present situation. It is well understood that there will be difficulties in placing it in practice, because any reform, even an excellent and beneficent one, must overcome obstacles. But . . . it is not necessary to exaggerate the obstacles: the decimal system is

not an abstract science; it is simple and clear, and to a certain point natural: Do we not see Indians, children of nature, counting on their hands and by twenties? Once we know the approximate correspondence of the old currencies with the new, the difficulty is half overcome, and the names of the pieces are not important: reales, medios or pesetas; little by little all will get used to them. It is the duty of the educated part of the population which understands the new system without difficulty, to make [help] the ignorant class, with which it is in contact daily, understand in order to smooth the transition: it is a duty imposed by patriotism. Nothing is difficult to good motivation. We may all remove the first stumbling blocks and not doubt that a reform will be realized that must exercise a powerful influence on the prosperity of our country.[17]

The monetary reform was carried out. In early December 1870 the government called for exchange of defective coins at the mint by January 31, 1871. For the most part the operation appears to have been managed effectively. However, the problem of acceptance by the lower classes of the decimal-based fractional currency — that is, the small coins of everyday use — was as difficult as some had feared. It is not clear precisely where the reluctance to use the coins came from, but undoubtedly it involved social habits and distractions related to the political revolution that came less than six months after the monetary reform. Before 1871 was finished, a new regime would accept the reform in general terms while retrenching some of its specifics. "The monetary law of September 21, 1870," it announced, "presents grave inconveniences because the country is not prepared to receive in all its applications the decimal metric system that forms its base." Despite the unquestionable advantages this system offered for accountability, it was clear that the binary division of the peso into reales and half-reales, to which the people had been accustomed, was more convenient for daily use. Observed the Boletín, "The public shows notorious repugnance for the decimal division of the monetary unit (peso) when it does not divide like the binary into reals and half-reals, while multiple decimals of the same unit have been accepted because they do accommodate better with the previous (binary) system."

This decree noted that the 1870 law reduced silver content in the fractional currency of the peso and that the coins' heraldry was not in harmony with the principles proclaimed by the nation — that is, by the revolution. Therefore it was decreed that fractional currency of the silver peso was raised from the .835 silver content established in the 1870 monetary law to the .900 silver that had been established as the intrinsic value for the whole peso. Fractions of the peso would again be divided on the traditional binary basis: either two coins worth four reales each, four coins at two reales each, eight coins at one real, sixteen coins at a half-real, or thirty-two coins at a quarter-real. Heraldry on some of the coins was also rearranged, including the inscription on two of them of "30 de junio de 1871," the date of triumph of the revolution.[18]

Land Reform

An improved currency would encourage the introduction of new capital into Guatemala, but just as important and more difficult to obtain was an improved system of land tenure. Modern capitalists could not be expected to loan money at favorable rates, secured by land, if land law created undue obstacles to mortgage foreclosure. Land was cheap in Guatemala, but there were several different modes of possessing it, and most of those provided only precarious title or titles of questionable merchantability. Much of the expansion in agriculture had been and would continue to be in coffee plantations. Considering that coffee trees took several years to reach productive age and then constituted an immovable asset, precarious title was unacceptable. If a foreign capitalist purchased land whose title could not be cleared for resale (i.e., was not merchantable), his capital was not secure because it might not be recoverable. In all, the Economic Society believed that a radical reform of landholding was required.

To promote this reform, in May 1870 the Society announced a competition to design the best plan "to make the land a secure guarantee for the capital loaned to agriculturists on the basis of land mortgages." Only two proposals were entered by the deadline on December 16, and neither was found adequate to the elaborate objectives of the contest, so a prominent local jurist was commissioned to draft an appropriate mortgage law. However, this process was not completed before the revolution.[19]

The mélange of land tenure involved land held in public and in private; by religious communities and diocesan institutions; by village *ejidos* and a variety of communal organizations; by traditional squatters and new squatters (none of whom had title documents); and by Indian *cofradías* and other Indian festival organizations. It included tracts with surveyed boundaries (*de extensión determinada*) and without survey. Above all, the legal status quo was a rich source of encumbrances to title that could not be easily cleared, and thus land sales and mortgage foreclosure were sometimes very difficult to carry out. According to the Economic Society, only one set of legal conditions provided the kind of title that agriculture needed: surveyed boundaries and a clear, marketable title that could not resist proper mortgage foreclosure. Not surprisingly, in June 1870 the licensing and training curriculum for surveyors was regularized by government decree.[20]

It does seem clear that the Economic Society best represented the progressive element within the elite. In late 1870 its writers argued implacably for modernization of agriculture — the country's basic source of wealth — and for modernization of any institution that blocked such a process. Their essays related money, interest, and land and distinguished between export agriculture and ordinary agriculture. As noted previously, one essayist called for repeal of the usury law of 1840 in simple nineteenth-century economic terms: Interest on money was merely another commodity and must properly respond to supply and demand.[21] Another essayist (also quoted previously) made the distinction between export agriculture and ordinary agriculture, noting that the coffee revolution changed the problem of feeding the country and required clear, responsible thinking.[22]

Jules Rossignon, a French immigrant coffee grower, prominent scientific agriculturist, and secretary of the Economic Society's commission on agriculture, circumvented press restrictions with a bitterly ironic essay that attacked less progressive elements, specifically old-style hacendados. He noted that some persons saw the role of capital in agriculture as a mystery — at the very time the Economic Society was sponsoring its mortgage-law competition to provide needed protection for capital. With school-primer precision, he pointed out that industry is based on capital, that capital is money, and that money pays for buildings, tools, workers, and so forth. Like other industries, he observed, agriculture needs these things and thus needs money — capital. "But there is capital and capital. The engineer who puts together an industrial plant buys coal, iron, steel, hires workers, commits an industrial act. The person who buys a great hacienda among us, does something that has no relation to industry." The person might decide not to put the property to agricultural use and merely experience the joys of being a great landowner; although his invested capital would not be productive, his vanity would be satisfied. Conversely, he might rent the hacienda to a farmer who would bring the material and labor necessary for planting and producing a harvest. The farmer would then be the true industrialist because he would provide the necessary working capital for production.

Rossignon summarized by distinguishing two kinds of agricultural capital, "property-capital and working-capital." The person who bought a hacienda without discerning how much of it could be cultivated would probably be in trouble because he would be confusing agricultural property and agricultural industry. If one concentrated on agricultural production, then one's capital would produce as much as that of the industrial engineer. "This is why we always see great fincas lose all their value the day they cease to be cultivated, [and] why it is so difficult among us to find money loaned on the value of a *property*, while the agricultural industrialist easily finds the capital necessary to devote himself to his cultivation." Land was cheap in Guatemala, but to attract foreign capital the government should attract the immigration of skilled foreign farmers who could turn unused lands into well-administered *fincas*. The great stretches of unused land on the traditional haciendas represented only imaginary capital.[23]

Rossignon's analysis and sentiments fit well with a different commentary on conflicts within the elite in that autumn of 1870, a pseudo-Darwinistic tract printed as a sententious editorial in the *Gaceta*. As part of its efforts to promote agriculture in the country, the government sponsored a new fair in Jutiapa to be held November 15. A month before the event, all was not going well, and the government called upon businessmen for the desired cooperation. If the obstacles inherent in launching such an event made it fail that year, it would be repeated and perfected little by little in future years. Urged the *Gaceta*, "We should all try to aid the supreme authority in the arduous task of looking after the common good. We should all look to the future and breathe its air. Each step on the path of progress is, in a literary sense, a divorce between the past and the future, the present serving as intermediary, a transitory modification between two extremes." Every divorce involves pain, argument, and protest; every achievement creates a problem as it opens new possibilities; struggle is necessary because there is resistance to change. The *Gaceta's* statement was particularly enigmatic because, although it appeared to be a rallying cry ("If there were no hostile forces, there would be no triumph"), it was pitched against "inertia and the vices that retard the improvement of peoples," forces that would exist for a long time. Those sounded like charges García Granados might hurl against Cerna.[24]

An End to Consensus

The *Gaceta's* call to mobilize, to gird for the long haul, probably resulted from the darkening political scene. Since its beginnings in 1865, the Cerna regime had worried about the triumph of Benito Juárez and liberalism in Mexico. Serious military challenges to the regime had been launched from

Soconusco and Chiapas since 1867. Thus, when it was learned at the beginning of August 1870 that Miguel García Granados had reached the northern borders of Guatemala by way of Mexico City and was organizing a new invasion by way of the two Mexican border states, the *Gaceta* expressed shock. Serapio Cruz had engaged in criminal and generally reprehensible conduct, but he had never dared to invade the country with foreign troops; "he did not wound national sentiment and independence to the quick." But García Granados, who had been allowed to leave the country under bond and upon his promise not to return to Guatemala or to disturb its public order, was now recruiting an army of invasion in Mexico. To do all this, said the government, he had made a pact with "the sanguinary [Rufino] Barrios and the other malefactors who accompany him." It seemed incredible to the editorialist, "more absurd than criminal," but the reports had been confirmed. "With what credentials would the new ringleader promote a revolution? Cruz at least was able to delude himself that he was adding prestige to his name and long service in defense of Guatemala; but in the present case, there is nothing, absolutely nothing, that can excuse such unfounded pretensions." Of the various harebrained attempts to overthrow the government, none had been so unwarranted and so universally condemned as that of García Granados.[25]

Six weeks later García Granados himself joined the debate by means of an open letter to *La semana* answering the government's early August attack. Since propaganda — persuasion of the elite — was the real objective of the debate, honor became an issue. He denied taking on Mexican officers, denied recruiting Mexicans or malefactors to invade Guatemala, denied promising not to make war on the government of Guatemala, and asserted that if he had done so under duress, such a promise would not have been binding. Certainly his honor would not have been involved in such a ransom. He noted further that every citizen had the right of insurrection against a tyrannical government.

The *Gaceta* responded that at the time of the fall of Serapio Cruz, the government had issued orders for the arrest of several individuals, including García Granados, because their political behavior endangered the republic. The writer added somewhat insensitively that the state had acted under the authority of the May 8, 1869, decree, which suspended constitutional guarantees, and had been supported in the action by the (now purged) Chamber of Deputies. The correspondence covering García Granados's banishment was reprinted, and two more columns of a very lengthy article elaborated the current situation. The government wished to show that García Granados was not a man of honor. It convinced the new U.S.

minister, at least, who reported to Washington that García Granados was an "archtraitor and consummate villain."[26]

For almost six months after this exchange, the government spoke little of events in Mexico and as much as possible about those "tutelar deities of nations, peace and order."[27] However, on occasion it considered Mexican actions so provocative as to require comment. On November 19 the *Gaceta* replied to a scurrilous letter published in the Mexican journal *Revista Universal* that reported Guatemalan invasions of Mexico. "How could that editor hide from himself that those false reports of Guatemalan invasions, already contradicted by the Mexican *Diario Oficial*, were spread by [Guatemalan] exiles joined with the mandarins of Soconusco and Chiapas?" the *Gaceta* asked. He was so incensed that he felt compelled to share with his readers this example of the calumnies spread from Chiapas:

> The Government of Guatemala is based on unpopularity, sustained by [religious] fanaticism, terror and monopoly, and its sons make war on it in all corners of that nation: its sons wish liberty and progress in the Mexican style; they proclaim this from the last hut of the laborer to the great salons of the potentates; and this echo, sustained by the arms of a member of its legislative chambers, Señor García Granados, as well as by Barrios, attempts to extinguish that government which has adopted as one of the methods of its harebrained program, sarcasm, insults, and vexations against the Mexican frontier region.

The editor responded by commenting on each element of the Mexican pronouncement, including a supposed Guatemalan desire for "liberty in the Mexican style," and asserted that these elements "exist only in the imagination of malicious individuals." He could not understand why a journal such as the *Revista* would allow its columns to be used for such fraudulent purposes.[28]

A week later President Cerna himself presented a positive interpretation of the developing crisis. He saw the foreign affairs of Guatemala as harmonious, aside from relations with Mexico and Costa Rica. He noted, perhaps as a tu quoque argument, the troubles of the two most "civilized" nations of the Old World in the Franco-Prussian War and hoped they would soon be able to achieve peace. Cerna's effort to project calm relations with Mexico was impressive: Public tranquility, indispensable to continued progress, had been preserved despite criminal attempts to disturb it. It was hard to overlook the unfriendly conduct of authorities in the neighboring state of Chiapas, who permitted frontier towns to be "converted into *foci* of hostilities and machinations" against a peaceful neighbor, then glossed over those proceedings by inventing complaints against the government of Guatemala to influence public opinion in Mexico. Guatemala had denied those calumnies and asked Chiapas officials to halt activities that were unjustifiable and prejudicial to towns on both sides of the border. "At last convinced of the uselessness of those steps, we have turned to the general government of that Republic [in Mexico City]. I believe . . . that the [Mexican government], free of the petty passions and squalid views that seem to inspire those who attack us from the neighboring state, will know how to put a stop to those excesses and make those authorities curb the exiles' political activities." Most important, unpatriotic attacks launched from Mexico would fail in the future as in the past because of the good sense of the Guatemalan people.[29]

In Central America only a suspension of relations with Costa Rica marred Guatemala's diplomacy, and that rift probably could not be commended as long as the Guatemalan archliberal Lorenzo Montúfar remained a member of the Costa Rican government. Probably Cerna was tweaking Montúfar, though not by name, when he suggested that relations would not be renewed until Costa Rica's government was inspired by a more just and liberal sentiment.

Expectations of an invasion from Mexico grew in the winter and spring of 1871, but writers in the Gaceta continued to advocate peace, order, and progress, which necessarily took place slowly in a country such as Guatemala. Praise of the Guatemalan people was also plentiful, rather in the manner of a parent attributing qualities to a child — in the child's presence — in hopes the child will develop such qualities. Typical of such effusions was one published on February 3, 1871, which held that Guatemalans possessed a delicate sense of good and bad and understood that "the present order of things" was adjusted to the reality that "development of the institutions and broadening of liberty" had to await the country's maturity if it was to avoid catastrophe.[30]

An adult education curriculum for artisans offered by the Economic Society provided a specific example of the regime's incremental pursuit of progress in 1871. Presented by the government to help members of the working class contribute more to the nation's development, this education was supposed to enable them to compete with their counterparts "in the countries of more advanced civilization." The classes for artisans were to open on April 15 in reading, writing, mechanical drawing, applied arithmetic and geometry, religion, morals, and urbanidad. "This is for now; later, when students have been prepared, elementary courses in applied physics, mechanics, chemistry and architecture will be offered," the *Gaceta* promised. Emphasis was placed on how profitable these free courses would be to the laboring classes: "These are the fruits of peace and order in a country where the great majority of the inhabitants, respectful to the established Government and the constituted authorities, is dedicated to developing elements which must bring culture and wellbeing, civilization and credit to the fatherland."[31]

Unfortunately for the government, the elite consensus in Guatemala City had broken down by this date. The semiofficial journal of the Economic Society openly discussed this disintegration in a series of articles charging the establishment with indifference to progress, whatever the claims of official spokesmen. Considering the importance the regime attached to appearances, this almost clinical statement of no confidence in the status quo must have seemed immeasurably harsh to hard-line conservatives. "Ignorance, egotism, lack of patriotism, the laziness of spirit which is called apathy, and sometimes even envy, are obstacles which hinder the march of progress in many countries," one article charged. "Some timid men tremble to hear the word 'progress' pronounced. For them progress is the equivalent of revolution, of anarchy." Yet all countries inescapably must obey the "natural and immutable law" of progress. The present generation had benefited from the civilization provided by those who went before it. Thus, all are obligated to work for society, preserving and augmenting the material, intellectual, and moral capital of mankind: "Progress is a note sent by our predecessors in favor of society, which we have the obligation to pay."

To transmit the inheritance from forebears to descendants, the society suggested, agriculture ought to get out of its rut and become truly progressive. It could do so by improving communication, cattle breeds, seed grains, labor practices, and the use of fertilizer. More broadly, expansion of primary education and practical instruction in industrial science would help, as would domestic supply of an expanded domestic market. Yet the writer concluded that very few persons were willing to cooperate or even to encourage the progressives: "The indifference in matters of progress is an epidemic moral infirmity." Opening a railroad in the republic had been advocated the previous year, but now no one agreed to it, and suspension of construction of the railroad in Honduras was met with indifference. A textile factory installed at great cost and effort in Antigua now got the attention of no one. An "ingenious" and practical device — the apparatus of the Frenchman Carré that could produce hundreds of pounds of ice under the tropical sun in a few hours — would soon cease to function in

Guatemala. "The electric telegraph with its extensive wires has remained confined in a corner of the Tax Administration office like an archeological curiosity or like an archive from the time of Carlos V!" the writer noted. "What can explain such a discouraging result except indifference in matters of progress?"[32]

These words came from Rossignon, a successful, experienced, middle-aged progressive who was prepared to concede that Guatemala had advanced during the preceding twenty years. They were seconded by members of the younger generation. Ramón Rosa and Marco Aurelio Soto were two of the many young Central Americans (Hondurans in this case) who left their homes to seek a university education in Guatemala City. Intellectuals who eventually identified clearly with liberalism, they had made a place for themselves in the progressive wing of the Guatemala City elite by 1869. Soto had become secretary of the Economic Society by 1870, and Rosa was writing major reform articles in its journal by 1871. The acceptance of these very impatient young men illustrated the breadth of the Cerna consensus; their strident dissent of early 1871 marked its dissolution. Rosa wrote a series of articles entitled "Legislation in Its Economic Relations" to set forth a number of his ideas. A Jesuit writer responded with an essay titled "Lending and the Medieval Theologians" in *La sociedad católica*, dissecting Rosa's work in a most negative way. Rosa's answer was erudite, aggressive, and essentially liberal. He had hurt the Jesuits' feelings, Rosa concluded, when he wrote that the epoch of the medieval theologians was "very sad." Rosa had cited Voltaire's expression "sacred contagion" to describe the religious fanaticism of those theologians. With sophisticated arguments, he made clear that he had been attacking their fanaticism, not the Middle Ages as a historical period. And he was very sarcastic about the Jesuits.

"That *liberty is the fertilizing medium of modern peoples*, is an incontrovertible assertion in the nineteenth century," Rosa observed. "Nevertheless those words have been underlined" (original emphasis). He challenged "the very Reverend Fathers" to show that political, religious, social, individual, civil, and industrial liberties were lies. They would have to demonstrate that people have not been regenerated in the modern age through liberty. They would have to prove that liberties were not recognized and practiced in an enlightened Europe, in the republics of South America, and "especially in the United States of North America, in that classic Republic, temple of liberty and seat of the greatest ideas." If the Jesuits showed all that, Rosa would retract his words and condemn himself to silence. "But while those facts stand, we shall repeat always: LA LIBERTAD ES LA SAVIA FECUNDANTE DE LOS PUEBLOS MODERNOS."[33]

Rosa published this reply to the Jesuits just as the final, military phase of the Revolution of 1871 commenced. A month later, with the final lines drawn, he was joined by his friend and cousin Marco Soto in another assault on the usury law and the Jesuits who advocated it. Their essay amounted to an indirect attack on the Cerna regime. The two actors saw the unfortunate results of Spanish mercantilism ("the protectionist system") to be immorality, poverty, and obscurantism. In contrast, they advocated positive, rather than restrictive, legislation: "The laws ought to support capital with solid guarantees, creating good credit institutions, seeking to maintain the value and mobility of property (*cosas*), encouraging work, and prosecuting vagrancy, overturning bad fiscal and mortgage legislation, reforming, in sum, the administration of justice, which, delayed, is a hindrance and harassment of individual rights."

Rosa and Soto concluded with another frontal attack on the Jesuits and the 1840 usury law that limited interest to 6 percent. This law, they said, was "anti-economic." The reverend fathers had piously declined to comment on the developmental results of allowing free interest rates because they lacked a "mandate" and the "competence" to do so. The young turks replied, "We believe this to be a republican community, where everything should be discussed, and where previous *competence* does not need to be declared, nor does anyone need a *mandate* in order to set forth what he thinks about social issues." Only oppressive governments decided on public matters, and only reactionary publicists taught the humiliating politics of abstention and silence. Those who were forthright and concerned should speak out, expressing their ideas. "In the United States of North America, which is the best governed country in the world, hundreds of newspapers are published in which everything is discussed . . . and the Yankees [declare] neither a mandate nor competence in order to speak of matters of common interest."[34]

The Revolution of 1871

By the time Rosa and Soto openly ridiculed Jesuit style in this fashion, the Revolution of 1871 was militarily under way. It had begun with Rufino Barrios crossing the border at Tacaná on March 28 with about thirty men, aiming to recruit more. For about six weeks the Cerna government assumed that the military effort of García Granados's movement would have the harassing character of the guerrilla raids that had occurred intermittently since 1867. Serapio Cruz had been the consummate guerrilla, involved solely in a war of attrition; Barrios, when associated with Cruz, had acted in similar fashion. Eventually, however, the government was forced to recognize, insofar as it was capable of doing so, that the new effort was different.

In 1871, at sixty-two years of age, García Granados was in a hurry. He knew the politics of Guatemala City with a master's eye. In the 1830s and 1840s, he had gained extensive military experience. He understood the Mexican political scene as well and was able to negotiate limited assistance from Mexican officials. Thus, his lieutenant, Francisco Andreu, was able to purchase repeating Remington rifles and import them through Tabasco on the Bay of Campeche, and García Granados could assign Barrios to transport those weapons from the Mexican port through Mexican territory to the Guatemalan border. This mission, and the lowland fevers that delayed Barrios, a highlander, from carrying it out for several weeks, provided one of the epic tales of the revolution. Naturally, Mexican officials resisted diplomatic pressure from the Cerna government to crack down on the revolutionaries. With all his qualifications and perspective, plus the realization that time was not on his side, García Granados conceived for his campaign the ambitious objective of capturing Guatemala City promptly, certainly not through prolonged warfare.[35]

Since it took officials in Guatemala City some time to understand the rebel strategy, García Granados's "Army of Liberation" outmaneuvered them easily. The government expected his small army, never more than a few hundred strong, to retreat to the mountains or to Mexico after a battle — which the government tended to see as a raid. But García Granados kept his eye on the capital, and any march not in the direction of Guatemala City was to him merely a brief detour.

There seems little doubt that the strategic concept of García Granados explains the short duration of the military campaign (three months, March 28 to June 29) and the complete victory it achieved. This concept held that a small and well-equipped military unit (which one writer even called a phalanx), with an excellent spy network and a propaganda campaign appealing to democracy and modernization, could outmaneuver and quickly defeat a stagnant regime that for years had been explaining away its refusal to enact any fundamental change.

García Granados's family history had prepared him psychologically for a campaign in Guatemala that required negotiated, halfhearted Mexican support. His father's trading career in Spanish Guatemala in the 1790s had featured trade through Chiapas and the Bay of Campeche rather than the ports of San José or Izabal. At least one older brother had lived permanently in Mexico as a businessman since the 1830s. García Granados had been involved in business there himself. He could be realistic rather than resentful when Mexican officials agreed unofficially to allow him to launch his campaign from Chiapas and Soconusco on the proviso that he not come back, on pain of being interned and having his Remington rifles confiscated. Although liberal Mexican officials liked the idea that the clerical-conservative regime of Cerna would be toppled, they did not want the kind of extended diplomatic exchange that had resulted from Cruz's years of border hopping.[36]

A detached view of García Granados's ninety-day campaign in 1871 can perceive in it all the elements of a desperate adventure story with a triumphant conclusion. He crossed the border at Cuilco (Tacaná) and Tapitzalá with the knowledge that it was his Rubicon, that he could not turn back. He had to gain sufficient notoriety and recruit and train sufficient men to become operational before the Guatemalan regime could focus upon its destruction. In the first two weeks, his lieutenant, Barrios, with an advance party seeking the first hundred recruits, hid out in such remote places as Trampa del Coyote and the heights of Serchil, which he knew much better than did the government.

But García Granados's strategy required frequent occupation of population centers so that he could issue quasi-governmental proclamations for propaganda purposes and so his force could assume the shape and project the image of a government. Given the tiny size of his forces, mere hundreds against the government's thousands, such a strategy meant that the insurgents had to move swiftly from place to place and keep out of the way of large government detachments until the right opportunity presented itself. Information on government plans and troop movements was, of course, crucial. The first major town occupied was San Marcos on May 8, taken without a fight because the government had withdrawn its garrison to nearby San Pedro Sacatepéquez, where political attitudes favored it.[37]

In San Marcos, García Granados issued a proclamation previously printed in Mexico. It explained his insurgency against Cerna's intolerable tyranny and carried a statement of injury, as well as other ideas that García Granados seemed particularly eager to lay before the public.

> *Fellow Countrymen:* Persecuted unjustly and illegally by the tyrant who governs the Republic, today I present myself to you with the object of regaining possession of my rights and of combating an administration that oppresses the people and daily violates the most sacred guarantees of man.

> For twenty years I fought that arbitrary and despotic Admini-
> stration, and if my efforts have not succeeded in overthrowing it,
> at least they have contributed efficaciously to publicizing the
> abuses, excesses and cruelties of the dictatorial system that rules us,
> thus encouraging Guatemalans to gather around the banner of
> liberty, to follow it and if necessary to defend it: this is why the
> tyrants hate me.

He described his private life in the capital in the preceding decades as
quiet and his role in the Chamber of Deputies as necessarily energetic. The
government of Cerna had not thought it prudent to attack and silence him
until the demise of Serapio Cruz. Then, in an act of naked tyranny, it tried
to throw him into the unhealthy dungeons of Fort San José. "Chance, or
perhaps Providence, saved me on that day," he said. He was sure the public
knew him well, and he knew that dictatorship could not make Guatemalans
happy, especially one as "cloddish and ignorant" as Cerna's. For their sake,
he made a public commitment to fight until it was overthrown and replaced
by the liberty of a government of laws. García Granados and the patriots
who accompanied him wished to eliminate "the so-called Acta Constitutiva, which is nothing more than an irregular and absurd document,
contrived with the view of establishing a dictatorship" with a small group
serving as its agents and satellites. The insurgents wanted "a true National
Representation, freely elected and composed of independent men." Such
a government would differ from Cerna's, which they saw, with few excep-
tions, as one of employees and opportunists.

As specific needed reforms, García Granados listed a free press, an
improved army, an organized public treasury, a just system of taxes, and a
national system of public education. Finally, all monopolies must go,
especially that on *aguardiente*; they were both wrong and ruinous to commerce and agriculture. Any intentions other than these attributed to his
cause would be slanderous, and his well-known ideas were not utopian. If
Guatemalans rallied to him against tyranny, they would be happy. He
pledged that his troops would not commit atrocities of any kind. Those who
felt constrained not to take sides in the struggle would be respected, but
"woe to those perverted sons" who went out of their way to oppose him.
Clearly he sought defections from the government, but he promised acceptance of those who merely sat on the fence.[38]

Both his plans and the danger of government attack dictated that
García Granados's column move out of San Marcos quickly, a pattern
repeated throughout the campaign. With less than two hundred effectives
at that point, he was driven by the need to move toward the center of the

country. He wanted to occupy Quetzaltenango immediately — it was the second largest city in the country and one whose population had historical grievances against the capital — but it was held too firmly. After firing on government troops near Cucho to publicize his new howitzer and Remington rifles, he descended from the mountains toward Retalhuleu, a significant agricultural center on the Pacific coastal plain that he reasoned would have a small garrison. He was correct — the government garrison moved out, and he was able to move in, welcomed by representatives of the city government.

But a trap had been laid. Before the day was out (May 14), the commander of the garrison returned with reinforcements, and a sharp clash ensued within the city. The importance of the incident, aside from the rebels' victory, was that Barrios proved his military capacity to García Granados for the first time. Barrios had not been impressive in the early recruiting effort and had shown himself to be insensitive to the political agenda of García Granados. The latter wanted to win over the people and become their champion while casting the government as their enemy; Barrios, until stopped, had forced villagers into the ranks. In Retalhuleu, however, Barrios saved the day. When the surprise attack occurred, bullets ricocheting through the streets, he rallied his troops instantly and, convinced he'd been betrayed by the city fathers after their effusive welcome, set fire to the town. Three hundred buildings were reported destroyed. If this did little for the insurgents' reputation, it helped at least to make their determination notorious. Though victorious in the skirmish, García Granados moved out the same night to San Sebastián and moved on hurriedly the following morning to avoid other surprise attacks.

Such swift movement was characteristic as the guerrillas moved along the western base of the mountains through the towns of Mazatenango, San Antonio Suchitipéquez, San José Ídolo, and Santa Bárbara, then headed into the highlands to Parramos in the district of Chimaltenango. This series of movements after San Marcos formed a circuitous route around the government field armies to the west, tending always in the direction of the capital. Parramos soon seemed unsafe, so the insurgent chief moved to San Martín Jilotepeque. The government could not believe this tiny force was really aiming at the capital, assuming that it simply wanted to reach the safety of the eastern mountains, as had Cruz. Actually, García Granados seems to have been dissuaded from taking an immediate, direct approach to Guatemala City by Rufino Barrios, who was not familiar with its current politics, did not think of the city as a ripe fruit ready to harvest, and thought the government army must be defeated in the field before an approach on the capital was risked. García Granados judged that the mere presence of a rebel army in the environs of the capital would paralyze it with hysteria.

Still, he was a skilled politician operating realistically in a desperate campaign. He strove for consensus among his field leaders. After his objectives and opinions were made clear, he sought and frequently accepted his lieutenants' counsel. Also, the further the campaign developed, the more he had reason to respect Barrios's tactical ability and rapport with the troops, and the more he relied on him. When, at Jilotepeque, Barrios urged a march back to the west to establish a provisional government there, probably at Quetzaltenango, García Granados agreed, although he feared that such a countermarch would be viewed in the capital as an insurgent defeat.

After a skirmish at Cucho, it became clear to the government that the raiders did not intend to go back across the border but rather were headed deeper into Guatemala. Lt. Col. Aquilino Gómez Calonge was assigned to catch and defeat them. His pursuit was sluggish at best, and he was hampered by Cerna's misinterpretation of the insurgents' strategy. When the rebels left Jilotepeque, Gómez Calonge thought they were heading for Santa Cruz del Quiché, and he left by the shortest route to surprise them there.

García Granados learned of Gómez Calonge's movements and decided to intercept the government column. The insurgents found a spot on Gómez Calonge's route, Laguna Seca, that was ideal for an ambush with their Remington rifles. As its name implied, Laguna Seca was a dry gulch that allowed them to set up a crossfire pattern. By now García Granados had three hundred effectives to use against Gómez Calonge's seven hundred. Surprise was complete, and the ninety-minute battle resulted in a resounding defeat for Gómez Calonge, who was fortunate to achieve an orderly retreat. He was aided by the reluctance of the rebels to pursue closely for fear of being trapped by a larger force.

The engagement at Laguna Seca on May 29 proved to be the battle that decided the war. The insurgents defeated a major government force more than twice their number, inflicting heavy losses upon it. The psychological consequences were profound on both sides. The rebels' triumph opened an immediate tactical opportunity to approach the capital. García Granados and Barrios agreed to test this opportunity and had marched to Antigua by June 1. Well received by officials there, García Granados learned quickly from his spies that Cerna was preparing an army reportedly six thousand men strong to crush him. On June 2, therefore, he began a strategic retreat from the vicinity of the capital, spending the night in Zaragoza and continuing on June 3 to Patzicía.

A council of war at Zaragoza decided to return to the plan to establish a provisional government in the western provinces at Quetzaltenango. Doing so would make the country's second city a magnet for support, force the government to fight closer to the Mexican frontier, and maintain a supply route to the exterior. Although this agreement with his counselors made sense, García Granados worried that it would allow Cerna to rebuild support in the center of the country. With this in mind, García Granados decided before reaching Patzicía to proclaim himself provisional president, even before establishing a provisional capital, in order to have a banner of legitimacy with which to attract immediate support and discredit Cerna. Publication of an enabling document now became important, and on June 3, 1871, it appeared in the form of the Acta de Patzicía.

In it, and on their own authority, the officers of the Army of Liberation declared the Cerna government a tyrannical oligarchy made intolerable to the nation through arbitrary cruelty and daily violence against the citizens' civil rights. Because Cerna had arrogated powers to himself not found in the law, he was a usurper; moreover, he had wrecked the public treasury by contracting the British loan at ruinous rates. The guerrillas refused to recognize the illegal Cerna government and demanded, in effect, its unconditional surrender. García Granados was declared provisional president and authorized to form a government immediately and a constitutional convention as soon as circumstances permitted.[39]

García Granados used the Acta de Patzicía as a propaganda device for recruitment and for structural purposes, presenting it to various towns for their ratification. Because a significant number of towns did issue declarations of adhesion and support, the device helped create an impression that the population was rapidly abandoning the government in favor of the insurgents. Virtually every town the insurgents marched through adhered to the Acta. On victory day García Granados would have in hand, in the form of these municipal declarations, a certificate of legitimacy for his provisional presidency.

Considering the massive army Cerna brought from Guatemala City on June 7 and the ease with which García Granados could move to the west, the time had come for the insurgents to establish a provisional capital in Quetzaltenango. They marched from Patzicía through a series of towns, including Totonicapán, experiencing no resistance at all. While in Totonicapán they learned that the *corregidores* of Los Altos districts had gathered in Quetzaltenango to oppose them, but on the road to Quetzaltenango, they learned that all government forces had abandoned the city by the coastal route. Therefore, the insurgents entered the capital of Los Altos on June 7, as Cerna left the national capital with the army that was to confront them.

In Quetzaltenango the provisional government spent four days absorbing local information, appointing new government officials for Los Altos, refitting the army, and decreeing laws designed to consolidate support for its cause in Los Altos. The most notable of these measures decreed full port status for Champerico, a natural outlet for Quetzaltenango. Previous efforts to establish the port had been abortive. Another decree, which directly affected the entire country, was abolition of the tobacco *estanco*. One facet of this decree — sale of all existing stocks of tobacco in government warehouses to the highest bidder — would provide immediate revenue for the provisional government. The third decree invalidated an 1860 tariff on cheap rum from Comitán, Chiapas. This action promised cheap liquor to those so inclined, annoyed the liquor *estanqueros* close to the government, and repaid the Comitecos for their hospitality while the insurgency was being prepared.

The Cerna government put forward its own propaganda with increasing urgency during the month between the insurgents' proclamation at San Marcos (May 8–10) and their triumphant occupation of Quetzaltenango (June 7). Through most of May the old technique was employed of contrasting the slow but sure policies of Cerna with the insignificance and bad character of the insurgent leaders, the latter being categorized with or below Serapio Cruz. The Battle of Laguna Seca on May 29 changed that. This major defeat of the government forces required explanation, and events moved much more quickly thereafter. As noted previously, the force led by Gómez Calonge had been surprised in an arroyo in a crossfire of repeating rifles. The lieutenant colonel made his report in Guatemala City the next day, and the government derived from him an explanation for public consumption: His unit caught the *facciosos* near Santo Tomás/Chiché and, having taken the best positions, began the attack. Though the troops were unfazed by the enemy's first fire, a sudden, inexplicable panic caused two or three companies that occupied the center to begin to disband. Despite major efforts to contain the disorder and to keep it from affecting the rest of the army, the dispersion quickly became general. The officers were able later to organize an orderly retreat. To government commanders the event remained inexplicable, because they calculated only five or six dead and about that many wounded. The government assured the public that it had plenty of troops in the capital and the departments to "pursue" the faction.[40] The same issue of the *Gaceta* reported the pleas of prominent citizens of Retalhuleu for aid to the three hundred families made homeless by the incendiarism of the *facciosos*, who "call themselves liberators of the people and promoters of its progress and welfare."[41]

To halt the political disintegration precipitated by the loss at Laguna Seca, President Cerna prepared to take personal command of the army in the field and issued to the citizenry almost his last general public assessment of the situation. He admitted that the malign faction had "shown some growth in recent days." These disturbers of the peace had occupied a few peaceful towns and treated them ill in passing through. However, the interpretive line of the government did not waver: "The tranquil and passive attitude which these and all other towns in the Republic maintain is an evident proof that the *facciosos* have not found anywhere the sympathies which perhaps they expected. The sentiment of orderliness and of adhesion to the established authority is profoundly rooted in the mind of the great majority of the country, laborious and tranquil."

In terms calculated to rally the oligarchy and without mentioning García Granados by name, Cerna criticized the insurgency as a weak and reckless abandonment of noblesse oblige. "Knowing the character and the tendencies of various top figures in that subversive movement, society is justly alarmed and understands how imprudent and culpable was the act of arming and exciting that destructive element which they cannot control even when they wish to, and that they are perhaps in danger of being its first victims." On this latter point Cerna played to a report from Antigua of Barrios bullying García Granados, a report published earlier with some relish by the *Gaceta*. He referred also to the well-publicized burning of· Retalhuleu, asking, "How can a revolution based on principles be started with arson, with the spilling of innocent blood, and with the destruction of private properties that the law has guaranteed?" The expense of raising an army would necessarily cramp the government's efforts at development, both fiscally and by reallocation of manpower. Yet Cerna indicated he would know how to meet his obligation to defend the country through "the authority that was commended to me, without my seeking it, and which I could not abandon in an epoch of disturbance and social danger." He cited directly the benefits of order and development made possible under the regime of the past thirty years.[42]

The journalism of alarm intensified. A government bulletin had reported on June 3 the brief insurgent occupation of Antigua. A careful count by a trustworthy witness indicated that the rebel army consisted of 315 men as it passed through Chimaltenango and reported destruction of the house of the corregidor and of the aguardiente deposit in that town. Similar events had been reported for Antigua in a manner calculated to alarm a conservative, elite audience.[43]

For the two weeks (beginning June 7) that Cerna took the field with the army, the government strove through its news bulletins to bolster resistance and counteract growing panic. On June 7 it reported that the insurgent Juan Viteri had made an unsuccessful fifteen-minute attack on the military barracks in Escuintla, southwest of the capital, and had gone on with fifteen men to join García Granados in Antigua. Simultaneously, it reported that in the far northwest the force of Vicente Méndez Cruz had approached Huehuetenango and had been scared off, going to Chiantla. It noted that García Granados had left Antigua on June 3 and headed northwest, destroying aguardiente and chicha works and extracting money from the towns he passed through. It called attention to a report that Rufino Barrios had criticized García Granados publicly in Antigua, thus suggesting that elites who put in with the ragamuffin insurgents could expect to be abused. When word came of the government evacuation of Quetzaltenango, a June 9 bulletin claimed that this action had resulted from a false report that the forces of both Méndez Cruz and García Granados were converging on the city. The report, however, was only too true: The rebels came, and insurgent occupation, destruction of the aguardiente works, and other outrages followed.[44]

The movements of Cerna were reported prominently as he passed through Patzicía, Patzum, and Sololá, where he was joined by Gen. Narciso Pacheco, who had evacuated Quetzaltenango by way of Mazatenango. On June 14 a bulletin analyzed the insurgents' Acta de Patzicía, dismissing town endorsements of it as having been made under duress. "The only significance of the act to which we refer is that Don Miguel García Granados has created on his own authority that circle of chiefs and officers whose names appear on it; and that these in turn have recognized him as General and Provisional President, claiming to invest him with the kind of dictatorship that supposedly knows no other restraint than his will." What else could be expected from such persons holding such principles?

By mid-June bulletins began to hint that a climactic battle was shaping up as Cerna approached Totonicapán, with the insurgents in Quetzaltenango apparently disposed to resist him there. A final lesson on the madness of revolution came in the Gaceta on June 22 in a lurid description of the fiery end of the Paris Commune, which had emerged during the Franco-Prussian War of 1870–1871. The post-war government at Versailles had finally crushed the commune in Paris, destroying an entire district of the city. The archbishop of Paris and many priests were reported to have been shot by the communists. The body count was impressive: 22,000 communists dead and 10,000 taken prisoner. Five hundred were going to the gallows daily. Various dispatches reprinted in the *Gaceta* painted a bloody apocalypse.[45]

The importance of espionage and sabotage as elements in the final clash of the revolution reveals much about the political situation. Cerna's cabinet, unwilling to let all ride on the marshal's proven military prowess, decided to "decapitate" the insurgency by recruiting four convicts as assassins to eliminate García Granados and Barrios. The four were sent to enlist in the rebel army. However, García Granados had been so successful at mobilizing discontent within the Cerna regime that someone on the government side betrayed the plan. Thus forewarned, the insurgents captured one of the assassins upon his enlistment and sent him ostentatiously to the firing squad. The other three disappeared.

As the last maneuvers for the climactic battle were carried out around Totonicapán and the insurgents moved to Tierra Blanca on the heights of Cochón (now Coxón), their final position, the insurgents counted coup again — within Cerna's army. A nephew of Barrios served undetected as a military aide of Cerna. He found an opportunity shortly before the battle to slip through the lines and give Barrios the entire plan of the government's army. The counterattack that was developed from this information, the superior field of fire of the insurgents, and the prowess of the Remingtons combined to bring the rebels a resounding victory in the Battle of Tierra Blanca on June 23, 1871.

Still, the rebel army was so much smaller (eight hundred men, maximum estimate) than the army of Cerna that it dared not pursue immediately. Learning that Cerna had indeed left the vicinity, the insurgents rested and celebrated on June 24, taking the road after him the next day. Cerna went to Antigua, where he was to be joined by reinforcements from Escuintla. García Granados again proposed bypassing Cerna and going directly to the capital, which he was now sure would be ripe for the plucking. Again Barrios demurred, insisting that occupying Guatemala City without first defeating Cerna's army decisively was simply too risky a procedure. They temporized. At dawn on June 29, García Granados and his staff went on a reconnaissance to the heights of Mixco, the bypass route he wished to take to Guatemala City, while Barrios remained in charge of the bulk of the army at the bivouac. Word came to Barrios of a dust cloud, perhaps caused by Cerna's army coming from Antigua. Barrios confirmed this information and marched toward San Lucas to challenge the enemy.

As at Tierra Blanca, Barrios placed his riflemen in elevated positions visible to Cerna's forces but out of effective artillery range.

Betrayal of Cerna, in the form of sabotage, was perhaps as critical at San Lucas as espionage had been at Tierra Blanca. The commander of Fort San José in Guatemala City had supplied gunpowder to the marshal's army. According to participants in the battle and in the subsequent government, the fort commander had, as Guatemalans say, "put goat meat in the tamales" — in this case by furnishing brick dust instead of gunpowder to some of the units. In the heat of battle, when Cerna's soldiers found that their weapons would not fire, they began to disband and to flee the battlefield.[46] This time Cerna was beaten for good, and he crossed the border into El Salvador. The commander of Fort San José was later appointed *jefe político* in Izabal by the new government.

The road to the capital now lay open to García Granados, but he wanted no pillaging and a minimum of disorder in the occupation. While he went about collecting and ordering his forces, the city council of Guatemala City had to deal with similar concerns and with the panic caused by the flight of Cerna, which left the city open to occupation by the insurgents. The council had two cards to play, and it played them well. First, García Granados was known to be devoted to civil process; second, Field Marshal José Víctor Zavala, an enormously popular figure and friend and cousin of García Granados, had remained in the capital when García Granados went into exile the previous year. Indeed, Zavala had made that happy solution possible when the Cerna government ordered García Granados's arrest, first by hiding him in his own home, then by persuading the British chargé to provide sanctuary, finally by helping negotiate the bond and exile. Thus, in the hour of insurgent victory, with most of the national government going into exile or hiding, Zavala became a resource of immense value to the city government, to García Granados, indeed to the country. The *cabildo* appointed him commandant of the capital department. Zavala provided order, and he led a commission of notables, including the diplomatic corps, out of the city to meet with the liberation army's provisional president to arrange a peaceful occupation of the city and change of government.[47]

Notes

1. Edwin Corbett to Lord Clarendon, No. 5, Guatemala, January 31, 1870, FO 15/147, 67–73.

2. Corbett to Clarendon, No. 10, Guatemala, February 21, 1870, FO 15/147, 88–95.

3. Corbett to Clarendon, No. 12, Guatemala, February 28, 1870, FO 15/147, 111–113; cf. Ministerio de Relaciones Exteriores, communications, Gaceta XVI, 56 (February 26, 1870), 11–12.

4. Ministerio de Gobierno, Gaceta XVI, 59 (March 21, 1870), 1; 61 (April 2, 1870), 1. Cerna, Acuerdo, Gaceta XVI, 62 (April 7, 1870), 3–4.

5. Cerna, Mensaje . . . a . . . la cámara, 5 abril 1870, Gaceta XVI, 62 (April 7, 1870), 1–3.

6. Exterior, Actos del Concilio, del Eco di Roma, 1 febrero 1870, Gaceta XVI, 63 (April 12, 1870), 5–6.

7. "El periodismo," tomado del numero 279 de El faro salvadoreño, Gaceta XVI, 67 (May 9, 1870), 3–4.

8. Memoria del Ayuntamiento de esta Capital, Gaceta XVI, 66 (May 3, 1870), 3.

9. "Agricultura," Sociedad económica II, 2 (August 1, 1870), 1.

10. R. C. [Ricardo Casanova?], "El interés del dinero," Sociedad económica II, 1 (August 1, 1870).

11. X & Z [Dr. Mariano Ospina?], "La sociedad católica," Sociedad económica II, 4 (August 31, 1870), 28–30, at 30.

12. Pastor Ospina, article from La semana (1868) reprinted as "Confusión monetaria" in Ignacio Solís, Memorias de la casa de moneda de Guatemala (Guatemala: Ministerio de Finanzas, 1979), IIIB (4), Capítulo 50, 955–974.

13. F. Hernández de León, "El atentado contra don Enrique Palacios," El libro de efimérides III, capítulo CXCV (Guatemala: 1930), 77–83; and in Gaceta XIV, 80 (July 22, 1865), 7. On Palacios's career see Gaceta XV, 3 (January 20, 1866), 4; 4 (January 29, 1866); Sociedad económica I, 2 (March 1866), 22; Gaceta XV, 97 (December 9, 1868), 774; Gaceta XVI, 43 (November 24, 1869); Gaceta XVI, 81 (August 25, 1870) and 86 (October 13, 1870), 2.

14. Decreto, 9 junio 1869, Gaceta XVI, 21 (June 19, 1869).

15. Ospina, in Solís, Memorias, 968.

16. "La nueva ley monetaria," Gaceta XVI, 87 (October 26, 1870), 1–4.

17. Ibid.

18. Ministerio de Hacienda, Decreto #37, Boletín oficial I, 21 (December 8 or 18, 1871), 2.

19. Sociedad Económica, "Concurso sobre el sistema hipotecario," *Gaceta* XVI, 67 (May 9, 1870), 2; Solís, *Memorias*, 900–902. Each entry in the competition was to contain an exposition of the mortgage law then in force; an essay on the difficulties and obstacles the standing law placed in the way of a secure guarantee for the lender and easy execution of the mortgage; an exposition of the proposed arrangements respecting acquired rights, which would eliminate those difficulties and obstacles; in sum, a draft law on the subject. The winning entry would be published by the Society, and its author would receive a gold medal and 300 pesos. The deadline was set at December 15, 1870. Maximum publicity was provided, with the three-column announcement of the competition published repeatedly from May through August. Concurrently, and no doubt as a part of the program to modernize the land-tenure system, the government decreed new licensing standards for surveyors that superseded the previous law of 1840.

20. *Ibid.*; Cerna, Decreto, *Gaceta* XVI, 74 (June 28, 1870), 1. See David McCreery, "State Power, Indigenous Communities, and Land in Nineteenth-Century Guatemala, 1820–1920," in Carol A. Smith, ed., *Guatemalan Indians and the State, 1540 to 1988* (Austin: University of Texas Press, 1990), 99 and 106, for discussion of the social and statutory situation of emphyteusis before and after Barrios's important decree of 1877.

21. R. C. [Ricardo Casanova?], "El interés del dinero," *Sociedad económica* II, 2 (August 1, 1870), 2.

22. "Agricultura," *Sociedad económica* II, 2 (August 1, 1870).

23. J. R. [Jules Rossignon], Secretaría de la Comisión Central de Agriculture, "Verdadero valor de las fincas rústicas," *Sociedad económica* II, 9 (November 15, 1870), 65 (lead editorial).

24. "La nueva feria de Jutiapa," *Gaceta* XVI, 86 (October 13, 1870), 2.

25. "Frontera de Chiapas," *Gaceta* XVI, 78 (August 4, 1870), 1.

26. "Un comunicado a 'La Semana,'" *Gaceta* XVI, 84 (September 18, 1870), 2–3; Silas A. Hudson (U.S. minister to Guatemala) to Hamilton Fish (secretary of state), Guatemala, February 16, 1870, FM 219, R 8.

27. "Situación," *Gaceta* XVI, 88 (October 30, 1870).

28. "La revista universal de Méjico," *Gaceta* XVI, 91 (November 19, 1870), 3.

29. Cerna, Mensaje, 25 noviembre 1870, *Gaceta* XVI, 93 (December 2, 1870), 2.

30. "Receso de la Cámara de Representantes," *Gaceta* XVII, 2 (February 3, 1871), 4; cf. "El progreso," 6 (March 3, 1871), 5.

31. "Enseñanza para los artesanos," *Gaceta* XVII, 8 (March 17, 1871).

32. J. R. [Jules Rossignon], "De la indiferencia en materia de progreso," *Sociedad económica* II, 17 (March 20, 1871), 129.

33. Ramón Rosa, "Algunas observaciones sobre el 'Préstamo y los teólogos de la Edad Media' artículo publicado in el periódico 'La sociedad católica,'" *Sociedad económica* II, 18 (April 22, 1871), 141–144.

34. Ramón Rosa, "Algunas observaciones sobre the 'Préstamo y los teólogos' . . . ," *Sociedad económica* II, 19 (May 11, 1871), 149–152. Apparently, this was the last issue under the ancien régime.

35. José Santacruz Noriega, *Gobierno del Capitán General D. Miguel García Granados* (Guatemala: Delgado, 1979), 33.

36. Miguel García Granados, *Memorias del General Miguel García Granados* (Guatemala: Biblioteca de Cultura Popular, 1952), vol. 1, chapter 1; vol. 3, chapter 2; vol. 4, chapter 8. See also Santacruz Noriega, *Gobierno del Capitán*, 51.

37. Santacruz Noriega, *Gobierno del Capitán*, 55; J. J. Peatfield (British acting chargé) to Lord Granville, No. 8, Guatemala, April 16, 1871, FO 15/148A, 93–96; and No. 10, May 16, 1871, FO 15/148A, 102–103.

38. Gregorio Contreras and Joaquín Díaz Durán, *Crónicas de la campaña revolucionaria de 1871* (Guatemala: Comité Central pro-Festejos de la Revolución de 1871, 1971).

39. Comité Central Pro Centenario, *Indice General de las leyes emitidas por los Gobiernos de la Revolución de 1871* (Guatemala: 1871), 193.

40. Boletín de noticias 10, 31 mayo 1871, *Gaceta* XVII, 23 (June 3, 1871), 2.

41. Boletín de noticias 9, *Gaceta* XVII, 22 (May 31, 1871).

42. Cerna . . . a los habitantes, 3 junio 1871, *Gaceta* XVII, 24 (June 8, 1871), 1.

43. Boletín de noticias 11, 3 junio 1871, *Gaceta* XVII, 24 (June 8, 1871), 2–3.

44. Boletín de noticias 12, 7 junio 1871, *Gaceta* XVII, 25 (June 11, 1871), 1; Boletín 13, 9 junio 1871, *Gaceta* XVII, 25 (June 11, 1871), 1; Boletín 14, 12 junio 1871, *Gaceta* XVII, 26 (June 15, 1871), 1. Cf. Peatfield to Lord Granville, No. 16, June 10, 1871, FO 15/148A, 119–121.

45. Boletín de noticias 16, 14 junio 1871, *Gaceta* XVII, 27 (June 18, 1871), 2; Boletín 17, 15 (?) junio 1871, *Gaceta* XVII, 28 (June 22, 1871); "Europa y América, noticias importantes," *Gaceta* XVII, 28 (June 22, 1871), 1–4.

46. Santacruz Noriega, *Gobierno del Capitán*, 79–80.

47. Wayne M. Clegern, "Transition From Conservatism to Liberalism in Guatemala, 1865–1871," in *Hispanic-American Essays in Honor of Max Leon Moorhead*, William S. Coker, ed. (Pensacola: Perdido Bay Press, 1979), 98–110.

5

Miguel García Granados, Provisional President, 1871–1873

As he took over the government of Guatemala, Miguel García Granados wanted a moderate result from the Revolution of 1871. A master politician under the old regime, he knew thoroughly the personalities, circumstances, and traditions of Guatemalan governance, and he had just won the greatest political gamble of his life. He chose, then, what must be described as a reformist course. It is equally clear that within a few weeks of the founding of the new regime, Rufino Barrios made impossible the kind of mild solution of Guatemala's problems that García Granados preferred. Barrios initiated radical acts against the status quo that vitiated the communal atmosphere necessary for a moderate solution, and the rest of García Granados's provisional presidency was compromised. Though he instituted a number of reforms, the provisional president would be distracted constantly by the need to deal with the political and military consequences of Barrios's acts.

Basic to this situation was the attitude of the Church, which intended to give up little or nothing of its privileged position. García Granados did not challenge this institution in the first weeks after victory. Rather, in the absence of any immediate conservative military threat, he made ostentatious use of the ceremonial structure of the Church to aid in stabilizing his regime. He would need such stability if he were to carry out liberal promises of freedom of the press, secular education, anti-monopoly measures, convocation of a constituent assembly, faster economic development, general revision of tax policy, and modernization of the military.

García Granados's moderation was defined by Barrios's radicalism and by the fact that the latter represented a growing segment of revolutionary opinion. At first it appeared that the moderates could prevail while accommodating the radicals. Three weeks after the insurgent army occupied Guatemala City, *La república*, a new weekly journal that supported García Granados and disavowed any political inheritance from the old regime, presented its ideology. Though in some ways radical, this ideology was acceptable to the new regime:

> Upon falling, the rotten edifice . . . turned into dust, and it has not even left ruins for rebuilding. And yet it is indispensable to begin building the Republic. . . . The Constitutional Act of 1851 and its additional act of 1855 are no more than decrees which erect a permanent dictatorship. There is no regular legislation. Who knows which laws governed, among those dictated in the last half century, or where they may be found; or, among the Spanish Codes still in force, which are the regulations that have been repealed or fallen into disuse? There is no public administration, . . . [only] lazy and absurd office routine. . . . There is no plan of public instruction. Suffice it to say that the University was ruled by ridiculous by-laws dictated by a Spanish magistrate whose ignorance is manifest in his work. There is no public spirit. How was it possible to have it when citizens were obliged to maintain inaction and silence for so many years? There is no republican tradition. And without traditions of this kind, the Republic is converted into a mere farce. In a word almost all the elements that are necessary for the functioning of a free, regular and progressive government are missing [from that inheritance].[1]

The writer perceived three important assets then available for building a real republic: the provisional government, which was "patriotic, prudent and pertinent"; the wisdom that enlightened and influential men, old and young, had derived from the disillusionments of the preceding half-century; and "the mild character of the great mass of the population, that accepts and obeys all that does not clash violently with those customs that have come to be second nature to them."

Eager to establish contrasts between old and new, this self-serving analysis ignored some real continuities. The new ideology assumed a gulf between social classes. The old regime had perceived that gulf also, though in terms of a tiny elite in danger of being dissolved in the masses. Each saw the Indians as untouched by progress, but whereas the old regime hinted that they were *perhaps* incorrigible (and thus proper wards of the state), the new perspective argued that they could *certainly* be reached by education and thus modernized. Both called for responsible, constructive, "true" progress. Spokesmen for the old regime held that this process required a firm footing in traditional social forms, whereas the new regime's spokesman in *La república* indicated that social forms must be modern to function in the modern world; traditional forms in Guatemalan politics, economics, and education were outmoded. Both interpretations claimed pragmatism and idealism as their basis. The old view feared irresponsible use of modern ideology that did not fit Guatemala; the new one feared that Guatemalan society would never measure up to modern ideology until it established properly modern forms.

State Versus Church

After the Cerna government fell, ecclesiastical affairs became the principal arena of contention. The conservative regime of thirty years had represented unity of church and state; under the new regime, separation of church and state, a basic tenet of liberalism, became a central and permanent theme. In Guatemala the Church had been so fundamentally involved in education, taxation, development, and welfare programs under the old regime that its disengagement from those temporal activities would be difficult. The archbishop, Bernardo Piñol y Aycinena, had an institutional obligation to defend vested rights of the Church, and he represented two of the four families that anchored the pre-1871 elite in Guatemala City. Thus, he served as a double target for modernizers who wanted to reduce institutions considered obsolete. For about six weeks after the liberal triumph of June 30, 1871, the archbishop and the provisional president cooperated cautiously. Then came news from Quetzaltenango that the local *jefe político* — who had replaced the *corregidor* of the old regime — had expelled the Jesuit order from that city. Clearly the expulsion had been directed by Barrios, who commanded the western district centered at Quetzaltenango.

Even if it was an immoderate act, expulsion of the Jesuits from Quetzaltenango developed logically from the revolution. Freedom of the press was one of the first liberal reforms declared by the new government. Under this measure a flood of pamphlets and broadsides appeared across the political spectrum, discussing issues of the day. Interest in religious reform, even "religious revolution," was reflected in many of these pieces. A lesser number of pamphlets replied, defending the status quo. Under the new law all political articles had to be signed, and the press was enjoined from attacking citizens' private lives. However, in the passion of the day, pseudonyms were used and private lives were indeed attacked. The exchange of ideas and particularly the ventilation of anti-clerical critiques proceeded at an unprecedented pace in Quetzaltenango as well as in the capital. In particular, the Barrios newspaper *El malacate* in Quetzaltenango unleashed bitter attacks on the Jesuits, who responded by petitioning the city council to stop those attacks.

Instead the council began to discuss the legitimacy of the Jesuits' residence in Guatemala. It noted that they had returned to the country in 1851, after having been expelled in the eighteenth century, on the basis of a presidential decree unsupported by legislative action. Further, instead of enriching education they had enriched themselves by trickery, fraud, and preferential treatment. The council concluded that General Barrios and the jefe político should send the Jesuits to Guatemala City to be dealt with by the national government. Other than the council's action and subsequent supporting statements from other town councils in the region, there is no evidence of a popular demand for expulsion of the order from Los Altos. It appears rather to have been an organized campaign by the Barrios faction that forced García Granados to make an early decision regarding the disposition of a dozen Jesuit exiles on his doorstep in Guatemala City. The Jesuits themselves had been forced to act on even shorter notice, having been notified at 9 P.M. on August 12 that they must leave at 3 A.M. on August 13.[2]

The archbishop learned of the situation about as early as the provisional president did and applied maximum pressure on the executive — by immediate personal interview and formal letter — to get the expulsion cancelled. García Granados played for time until he could learn the circumstances and then concluded, despite his irritation at the unauthorized act, that he must support Barrios's decision. He needed the general's military vigor and his following and thus had to accept in some degree his radicalism. The government put the best face on matters in a supplement to the *Boletín oficial* (which replaced the *Gaceta*), explaining, "This somewhat violent measure has been criticized by some persons here, with all the natural bitterness of those adhering more or less openly to the past administration." The *Boletín* indicated that pro-clericals must accept the consequences of having invested their political capital in a dictatorship: "We would ask those who in their reactionary way invoke the guarantees of the Constitution, what constitution is it of which they speak?" This point coincided with *La república*'s earlier argument that when the old regime fell it left no viable democratic institutions.[3]

Caught between pamphlet attacks on the Jesuits, which urged the national government to expel the entire order from Guatemala, and scandalized objections from the Church hierarchy and its sympathizers, García Granados faced the crucial decision of his fledgling administration. A conservative uprising in the Santa Rosa–Chiquimula area precisely at this juncture may have been decisive. The disturbance could not be quelled by local officials and required the dispatch of an expeditionary force, which García Granados asked Barrios to command. The presence in the capital of all of Guatemala's Jesuit personnel, seventy-two strong, some already in a status of quasi-expulsion, agitated all sides. In this situation the provisional president could find no middle ground and decided finally to go all the way with Barrios and the *juntas patrióticas* that operated as the public claque of the radical liberal faction.

On September 3 García Granados ordered the Jesuits to leave the next day for San José on the Pacific. From that port they were to take a steamer for Panama. Silas Hudson, the U.S. minister in Guatemala, intervened to obtain a three-day delay on humanitarian grounds, arguing that preparations for exile required that much time. Preservation of law and order was essentially the only public explanation García Granados offered for the expulsion. That ground was ample enough to encompass both malignant agitation in the capital and an uprising in eastern Guatemala (the Oriente).[4]

García Granados might describe the Jesuit expulsion as an extraordinary event, implying that it was forced upon him by a ham-handed subordinate, but the subsequent dispatch of General Barrios to put down the unrest around Santa Rosa and the continuing press and pamphlet attacks on Catholic clergy clarified post-revolutionary reality in Guatemala. The relationship of church and state had been altered, despite all the protests of the archbishop and the maneuvers of García Granados to soften that harsh reality. The Santa Rosa revolt served as the main excuse for the Jesuit expulsion, with the Jesuits being blamed for the trouble. After hard-fought battles, Barrios put down the revolt in the battle of Cerro Gordo, September 23–24, 1871. Meanwhile, press attacks on the Church continued, the juntas patrióticas and *El malacate* being the main offenders as far as Archbishop Piñol y Aycinena was concerned. He recoiled in horror and in print when the junta patriótica of Amatitlán criticized García Granados for offering clemency to the "religious fanatics" in Santa Rosa who had provoked the local revolt. In rebuttal, the archbishop suggested in a letter to the government dated October 2 that the Jesuit expulsion was an attack upon religion itself.[5]

The government ordered the archbishop expelled from the country on the night of October 17. It justified this act on the grounds that the archbishop had shown partisanship in favor of the eastern uprising by refusing to publish a pastoral letter exhorting all believers to respect the civil authority and by not removing parish priests who advocated rebellion. In sum, the archbishop and the bishop of Teya, Mariano Ortiz Urrueja, were accused of inciting the rebellion and showing hostility toward the government.[6] An immediate result of their expulsion was that Father Francisco Espinosa y Palacios — a relative of Enrique Palacios — became governor of the archdiocese in the absence of the archbishop. Espinosa seemed to try to cooperate with the government that autumn, as the cemeteries and the university were secularized. However, the next major change the government forced upon the Church was one that Espinosa would pass on to Rome.

On December 22, 1871, the government decreed abolition of the ecclesiastical tithe, a 10 percent income tax, as of January 1, 1872. The government informed Espinosa on December 11 that it wished to end that tax because of the difficulty in collecting it and suggested funding the Church by other methods. The government offered to provide a fixed amount of 20,000 pesos per year in addition to the 4,000 pesos it had been paying since the Concordat of 1852. The 24,000-peso total would be secured by a one-half percent import-export tax. It was promised that these funds would be dedicated separately from the general budget, and the fixed amount would protect the Church from yearly fluctuations of income. Under time pressure from the government, the ecclesiastical *cabildo* completed its review of the proposals by December 15. Its major request, denied by the government, was that the matter should be referred to Rome.

García Granados's decree eliminating the tithe was direct and well received in some quarters. Some municipalities had asked for suppression of the tithe, and all resisted payment as being unjust because it weighed on a single segment of society, the agricultural and herding class. It was hateful because its collection always was disturbing, and civil authorities could not provide the support to make its collections effective. Yet the Church and related institutions had social obligations "that did not permit elimination of the tithe monies without replacing them in some manner." The local religious establishment agreed with the arrangement the government had proposed but was bound not to sanction it by Guatemala's concordat (treaty) with the Vatican. Thus, on its own authority, the provisional government declared the tithe suppressed.[7]

El crepúsculo, a liberal journal dedicated to support of the García Granados government, asserted that Guatemalans would celebrate this worthy act by a liberal and progressive government. Its editor noted that García Granados had resolved early on to be rid of the oppressive tithe, which had been borne only by the agricultural population.[8]

The ecclesiastical cabildo was not the only spokesman for the Church during the revolution. On the one hand there were priests such as Father Angel Arroyo, close friend and confidant of the radical Barrios. On the other stood priests such as Raymond Furcade, curate of Mazatenango, who were outraged by the expulsion of the Jesuits, the suppression of the tithe, and the bullying tactics of Barrios's men against priests who dissented from acts of the liberal government.

The case of Father Furcade, whose French name and formalistic style of debate suggest that he was a European immigrant, is significant as an early clash of Barrios's radicalism with an older cultural standard. Father Furcade was arrested at the local convent as he sat down to dinner in the early evening of December 22, 1871. Furcade suggested that he would be ready to go with the soldiers after dinner. Apparently this gesture of defiance enraged the commander of the detail; Furcade was assaulted, dragged from the building, and thrown in a dungeon (*calabozo*). In late January, Furcade had been released and expelled from the parish but still burned with "just indignation." He went to Guatemala City and sought out Field Marshal José Víctor Zavala, minister of war, and subsequently addressed to the field marshal an open letter requesting a remarkable degree of *noblesse oblige*:

> In regard to myself, Señor, I do not have any other politics than the Cross; my liberalism consists in helping the poor, and above all the humble poor, in repairing churches and convents with my money, in celebrating religious functions with the alms that they wish to give me; in preaching primarily against drunkenness, idleness, and the gushing of pettifoggers, who are the plague of the villages, the gossips and the calumniators. These are my crimes, and for these crimes no doubt General Barrios has committed against my person an enormous and unjustifiable assault, for which I ask corresponding satisfaction, and I take the liberty of supplicating you to request it in my name from the President, pointing out to him that I ask also for those of my parishioners who have been insulted in the most gross manner, jailed, and even muzzled, in the

name of liberty; pointing out to him finally that in Mazatenango
the rule is to protect criminals openly and to oppress good citizens.[9]

Whether personal or corporate in origin, this public letter was probably
the most bizarre effort by any member of the clergy to create a radical/mod-
erate split among the liberals. Zavala was somewhat to the right of García
Granados politically, whereas Barrios was far to the left of the president.
The response from Barrios's journal, El malacate, was immediate and
strenuous. It published a letter from the two ranking soldiers of the detail
that had arrested Furcade. They said they would not try to answer the
charges of Furcade; their specialty was the use of weapons on the field of
honor, not Latin quotations and other jargon displayed by the high-toned
priest. Instead, the soldiers simply said what they felt and indicated what
kind of person Furcade seemed to be. The result was vituperation. "The
celebrated and idiotic Furcade, in an undated letter to Marshal Zavala . . .
indulged in the inconceivable madness of offending our worthy chief
General Rufino Barrios. . . . His is the first devilish tongue to speak ill of
our worthy chief [publicly]." They thought it barbarous to mention General
Barrios and Furcade in the same breath on matters of honor. Whereas they
considered Barrios a valiant statesman and humanitarian, they described
Furcade in various postures as vermin, snake, poisonous reptile, bandit, and
pestilent garbage who had lived publicly in sin in Mazatenango!

The soldiers noted the awkwardness of Furcade's claim to special
clerical status but added that "there can be no remedy when the turkey
attacks the hunters." They thought it immensely ironic that one who
fleeced the poor with standard benedictions and chants wished to attack a
patriot for his methods. They indicated that if one could believe Furcade,
one could believe that cats were liberals! As to Furcade's desire for satisfaction, "If Don Rufino gave you satisfaction it would be 200 lashes (palos) in
the middle of the plaza."[10]

Formal response of the Barrios faction to Furcade's pamphlet came in
an editorial by Andrés Telles, close associate of Barrios and editor of El
malacate. He saw Furcade's jailing as far from arbitrary, but rather as a direct
result of his preaching sedition: "Is it not certain that in Mazatenango you
preached non-obedience to the provisional government, saying it was a
government for a few days only?" Further, the beating of Furcade was an
ordinary use of force that resulted from his resisting arrest. When he refused
first to leave the convent and then to go to jail, a sergeant picked up a stick
and gave him a few pragmatic whacks; Furcade then ceased resistance.
Telles went on to dispute a series of Furcade's charges, including his use of

Scripture. He pointed out that the most serious political act by Furcade was nothing less than "setting the provisional government and Lt. Gen. Barrios against each other by advising the punishment and firing of the latter worthy chief." Thus he was seen to have tried to introduce a schism in the Liberal Party.

Telles stated firmly that neither Furcade nor anyone else would be able to drive a wedge between the provisional government and Barrios. García Granados knew Barrios well and had complete confidence in him. Barrios, for his part, did not occupy his position as commanding general of the west out of ambition or need but because "that was where the government needed him to be." He noted that Furcade's letter concluded with "pure absurdities," particularly his use of the colonial title of curate (*cura*) for parish priest, a term Telles deemed worthy of "Cerna and his ministers to describe their past employment in the Republic." This statement suggested that *parroco* would be the correct, modern term for parish priest in the post-revolutionary period and that Cerna's government had possessed the character of a caretaker. Telles concluded contemptuously with the good news for Furcade that "he can write all he wants against General Barrios, being aware that the poisonous saliva he spews at the heavens will drop back in his face."[11]

The Furcade affair is important for the way its language reveals passion and intellectual presuppositions. Furcade had made himself known to the revolutionaries by the summer of 1871, and the uproar over his open letter to Zavala was merely the climax of his case. He had conflicts with the local jefe político in the first weeks after the liberal victory when he complained to the archbishop that the civil official was restricting his rights to preach and to converse privately. Even then, Father Furcade had expressed a grand view of the nineteenth-century struggle between church and state. With full theological argument, he had seen separation of the two as the basic problem. He portrayed God as the true life of the state, asserting that all kinds of misfortune resulted from a denial of this truth. In more pragmatic terms Furcade believed his troubles with the revolutionists began with a woman he had admonished for immorality. She reported falsely on a funeral sermon he had given for a dead soldier of Cerna's army before the triumph of the revolution.

The Furcade affair is most significant as a reflection of an extensive struggle between the church and state at the local level. Church archives have revealed serious friction at this level, though most cases were not as celebrated as that of Furcade; indeed, many were not even noticed by the central government.[12]

In 1872 and 1873 García Granados would twice place Barrios in charge of the government as interim president while he himself, despite his age, led an army into the field against reactionaries in the Oriente and in Honduras. Most of the initial legislation on ecclesiastical reform was established by Barrios during these interim periods and later accepted by García Granados. This legislation nationalized Church properties, outlawed religious orders, declared freedom of religion (*consciencia, cultos*), and suppressed the ecclesiastical *fuero* (special legal privilege for church personnel). This process essentially paralleled that which had earlier expelled the Jesuits. Only one major reform, suppression of the tithe, was initiated by the government while García Granados was presiding in Guatemala City — and, as noted previously, Church funding lost was replaced at once from other sources. Expulsion of the archbishop and the bishop of Teya two months before the tithe matter came to a head was an important, strong executive action, but it is better described as a startling change of policy (specifically, willingness to declare the head of the Church persona non grata) than as a reform.[13]

General ecclesiastical reform — that is, the breaking of the secular power of the Church in Guatemala — was the central change brought about by the Revolution of 1871. It was the lever for an irreversible shift toward modernization. Separation of church and state meant that direct recourse to Spanish institutions and values would no longer be available to a government unless it filtered them through nineteenth-century currents of thought. Spanish imperial institutions usually could not pass such a test. The earlier effort to bring about this kind of ideological and institutional shift had failed in the 1830s, but by the 1870s such a movement proved to be irresistible.

After a flurry of anti-clerical legislation, *Crepúsculo* published a series of strongly anti-clerical articles by the Spaniard Julio Álvarez Guzman in the summer of 1872. Mostly discussions of previous European church-state struggles, they complemented 1872 Guatemalan editions of Mexican reform literature by José Luís Mora (*Disertación sobre bienes eclesiásticos*) and Nicolás Pizarro (*Catecismo político constitucional de la República Mexicana*), as well as a reprinting of the Frenchman F. Laurent's *Secularización de la iglesia*, which justified expropriation of Church properties. The Church fought back with such pamphlets as *Observaciones sobre el folleto titulado "Secularización de la iglesia,"* which critiqued Laurent.[14] This activity was an expression of the elemental struggle in the press between radical liberals and the Church. The fight involved decrees in October 1871 excommunicating anyone who read *Crepúsculo* and similar promises in April 1872 for anyone who read *El malacate*.[15]

Probably the most intensely political charge made by the Church in this intensely political arena dealt with freedom of religion. The archbishop, speaking from the safety of unhappy exile, charged in April 1872 that *El malacate*'s article of March 8, 1872, "Libertad absoluta de Cultos," and other articles in the press advocating freedom of religion actually showed a preference for Protestantism. Denying such bias, the editor of *El malacate* responded that the point had merely been that Protestant ministers were, on the whole, more virtuous personally than were Roman Catholic priests and went on to parody the archbishop's letter. The government of a Roman Catholic population had to be sensitive to this issue and in fact had issued a public directive that jefes políticos should assure the people that the government was not trying to destroy traditional religion and warn them not to be distracted by rumormongers.[16]

Constitutional Assembly

The original demand for reforms under García Granados, as indicated by *La República* in July 1871, had not even mentioned the Church. Rather, the reform litany comprised representative government freely elected by "appropriate" voters, complete separation of powers, alternation in high offices (including no re-election of the president), well-defined responsibility for cabinet ministers, a free but responsible press, no monopolies in trade, academic freedom, equality of all citizens before the law, inviolability of domicile, and no punishment except by law. *La república* called immediately for a constitutional assembly, as a provisional government could not assure all of these measures.[17]

The peak and decline of García Granados's presidency occurred in the constituent assembly, which he called in December 1871 and which convened in the spring of 1872 following election of its deputies. Convened soon after exile of the archbishop, the assembly fit García Granados's moderate philosophy in that it sought an early establishment of representative government. It also provided an opportunity for extended interaction between Guatemala City conservatives, his own associates, and the radicals who followed Barrios. Actual debates of the constituent assembly were not completely reported in the *Boletín oficial*. But both the *Boletín* and *Crespúsculo* in the winter and spring of 1872 were talking a relatively conservative game. The U.S. Constitution was cited as a model, much as the Chilean conservative constitution of 1833 had been lionized during Cerna's time.[18]

An editorial in *Crepúsculo* indicated that Guatemala was caught up in a Latin American revolution of rising expectations. It also analyzed with some cynicism the different interests represented in the constituent assembly, saying: "Today Guatemala traverses a true crisis." It could not have been otherwise after the overturn of a regime of thirty years. The national situation was seen to be related inevitably to the special conditions of Hispanic America, the general character of modern civilization, the march of ideas, and the spirit of the century. Changes in all these areas conspired to create needs and make difficult their satisfaction. Such embarrassment and new dangers indicated that this was "one of those periods to which Providence subjects the world to make it pass to a new stage" unperceived by weak humans. "[Lamartine says] there are epochs in the history of mankind in which withered and dry leaves fall from the tree of humanity and in which aged and spent institutions sink by themselves to give place to a new sap (*savia*) and institutions by which rejuvenating ideas change the face of peoples."

The *Crepúsculo* editor saw the events of 1871 in grand terms, comparing them to the post-war scene described by Bolívar. There were those who fought for victory and then wanted their reward, he noted; there were those who did not aid the struggle yet afterward intrigued for high posts; and finally there were defenders of the old regime who resisted the resulting reform, demanding the fallen one as the necessary solution. In this situation the new provisional government needed the help of all men of good will.[19]

The provisional government now took the position, in all its hortatory and meliorative stances, that order must come before progress if the latter were to be achieved. Any revolution required time to adjust to peculiar conditions, and first things must come first. "The supreme government, meanwhile, moved by the noble desire to improve the condition of the people, [and] obeying the unavoidable laws of progress, is introducing in all branches [of administration] the reforms indicated by experience to be most necessary. . . . Peace and order, it has always been said, constitute the foundation of public welfare."[20] Thus, in the next issue of the *Boletín*, there came both an anti-sedition decree mandating exile for anyone inciting rebellion against the government and an assertion by the assembly that the first stage of the revolution, carried out by a small intrepid band, had been a "positive triumph for the nation; because it gave a severe lesson to partisans of personal and absolute governments, demonstrating to Guatemalans that despotism is impossible if the people know how to defend their rights."[21]

The *Boletín* was beginning to sound as cautionary as had the *Gaceta* before the revolution. It held that all fair-minded citizens could agree that the present government wanted to do well by them and that the spirit of the century, although eliminating many past errors of society, also had accustomed the public to expect prodigies as a matter of course. "Yet the work of progress remains slow and difficult. That which is achieved only through sacrifice and long periods of time in countries of greater vitality and of more abundant resources, we well know cannot be reached here in a day." Guatemalans would merely make themselves ridiculous if they expected instant reform of society and, worse, would compromise the positive things that had been accomplished in the field of welfare and culture. "It is truly surprising to meet those who may ask why this or that empty space has not been filled, one or another inconvenience remedied, this or that work undertaken." In its first stage the government would do well if it merely maintained order and established a legal regime.[22]

Another indicator of the government's moderate position was an editorial on constitutional law published in the *Boletín* in May 1872. The article commented on a reprint series based on the French constitutional experience — "a luminous writing whose publication is judged of undeniable utility for the project of a political code with which the constitutional assembly is now occupied." A principal conclusion of the series favored bicameralism, because inclusion of a senate provided a more balanced view of legislation.[23]

After a few weeks of discussion in the assembly, a seven-member committee was charged with preparing a constitutional draft in the summer of 1872, and the assembly adjourned on May 25. The document was complete by early August, and the assembly was called back into session on August 20 to continue its deliberations. Apparently the committee represented the views of the conservative wing of the assembly, because its draft, presented on September 9–10, brought a storm of opposition. Crepúsculo reported: "The draft, which had only two or three active defenders, was rejected by a majority so large it is impossible to doubt that the Assembly wants a more liberal constitution, which will satisfy the aspirations of lovers of genuine republicanism, not a law contrary to the principles fought for by patriots in the recent revolution to recover rights lost for so many years." The paper argued that the disapproved project embodied privilege for a mutually supporting oligarchy and theocracy: "Whether the reactionaries and their sycophants like it or not the majority of Guatemalans want to live under institutions that promote the progress of ideas, equality of rights, and delineation of duties of public functionaries."[24]

A new committee was formed, composed of Arcadio Estrada, who represented the García Granados faction, young Ramón Rosa, who at that point might be termed a liberal ideologue, and Antonio Salazar, a moderate who tried increasingly to accommodate the radicals. The editorialist in *Crepúsculo* approved of starting over with a new draft because he wanted the republic to be founded on true "liberty, order and progress" and not to constitute "the vile toy of a few aristocrats and ecclesiastics and their sycophants." He was certain the new committee would do better in meeting the desires of the assembly because "they have benefited from the discussion which the first suffered."[25]

In the autumn of 1872, while the new liberal draft was being written and presented, the conservatives made another play for public opinion against a constitution that seemed radical to them. Antonio Cruz thought the new draft went much too far. He noted that the first draft had been attacked for being undemocratic (*servil*) and for failing to meet the high aims of the revolution. But Cruz thought it should have been corrected rather than thrown out. He asserted piously that preparation and discussion of the new draft would extend the "dictatorship" — that is, the provisional presidency — for at least two months. Cruz had not yet seen the new draft but did not like some of the features he had learned from hearsay — the manner of electing judges and of dissolving the legislature upon a vote of no confidence. To Cruz it appeared to borrow too much from the British system and seemed monarchical, anti-republican, and dangerous.[26]

Already, however, the dominant coalition had spoken through *Crepúsculo* in the most combative terms against those who wanted to go slowly. The new constitution must recognize that, in essence, all the laboring citizen needed was that there be no privileged class.

> We ask . . . when has the conservative party ever proposed spontaneously any measure designed to promote the welfare or to broaden the power of the great popular mass? Who has done so? . . . The liberals, the men of progress.
>
> Now that Guatemala has placed itself on the right road, thanks to the sacrifices of the liberals . . . the conservative oligarchs and theocrats wish, with admirable aplomb, to make the people believe that they are the patriots par excellence, the champions of morals and religion, of order and of the general well being.[27]

It seems clear that García Granados lost control of the political process after November 12, 1872, when the assembly reconvened to consider the second constitutional draft. One Guatemalan historian asserts that rejection of the draft was immediate and stormy, that despite drastic amendments proposed by those who wished to save it, it never had a chance. Two blocks of votes became clear in the debate, one of centralists (*gobierno fuerte*) and one of democrats (*administración con poderes equilibrados*). As García Granados observed this process, he lost hope of obtaining a constitution during his interim administration. Faced also by press attacks against him, the old campaigner stunned the assembly at the end of December with his resignation. Unprepared, his opposition had to join ranks with his supporters and reject the resignation, which amounted to a vote of confidence. In mid-January the assembly voted a cash indemnity to García Granados (70,000 pesos) and to Barrios (50,000 pesos) for their personal losses in leading the Revolution of 1871. García Granados would handle his slide from power in the next five months in this typically adept manner.[28]

Military Reform and Modernization

By the end of 1871, when García Granados and Barrios had been in power for six months, it remained obvious to both that the problems of Guatemala's military establishment could be solved only through modernization. Early crises of the new regime had prevented the leaders from addressing such traditional and primitive procedures as the press-gang (used to forcibly detain men for military service). However, on October 24, 1871, it had already eliminated much of the *fuero de guerra*, the legal privilege exempting military personnel from civil courts in favor of military tribunals. The elimination of this exemption was limited to civil or military offenses committed outside the line of duty. Some liberals thought the remaining *fuero militar* should apply only to crimes of a military nature, not to common offenses, wherever they might be committed. The usual arguments were raised that justice could not be done if there were different jurisdictions for the same offenses.[29] Amid many such arguments, during the year 1872 the government proceeded to legislate a new military regimen, one it considered to be modern.

Early in 1872 *Crepúsculo* devoted a lead article to the military recruitment problem, pointing out that techniques used in the past were in every way unacceptable: "The system of incorporating in the army, in periods of disturbance . . . all the youths who could be seized by the patrols charged with such odious labor, is unjust and cruel and at the same time prejudicial not only for the individuals recruited in that way, but to the country in general." Field Marshal Zavala, had in earlier years repeatedly suggested to Presidents Carrera and Cerna that they introduce a system of enlistments, but his suggestions had not been followed.

Now the provisional government proposed a voluntary enlistment system for military companies located in the departments of the Center and of the Oriente: Bachelors of good physique between eighteen and thirty years of age could enlist for four years and receive a 20-peso bonus. This seemed a progressive step away from the previous system. To the editor of *Crepúsculo*, this proposal seemed good evidence that the government was interested in the well-being of the soldier, so important and so deserving of the country's support. He alluded to the sad fact that troops destined for hot, unhealthy ports were recruited from healthy parts of the country. In those ports, particularly San José, a man could quickly become ill as a result of hard service and little food (a situation that resulted from a low living allowance and high food cost). Beyond those difficulties, San José was short of good water, so the unfortunate person assigned there, if he did not perish from the miasmas of the coast, returned to his home with his constitution undermined, not to rest or work but to experience an early death. "Thus," the editor concluded, "many villages of the Republic are decimated by a process which deprives them and their economy of their healthiest men." This problem could be corrected by providing the soldier with healthy living quarters, practicing the strictest hygiene in those quarters, and recruiting men from coastal areas for duty at the ports.[30]

As months passed the new voluntary enlistment program failed to solve recruitment problems, and in June 1872 Rufino Barrios, as interim president, established a national military draft. It provided that all male citizens and permanent residents over eighteen years of age, without distinction as to class or person, had an eight-year military obligation. All must register for the draft. Government personnel, teachers, students under twenty years of age, the religious, the disabled, transient foreigners, and anyone who would pay 15 pesos per year for the privilege were exempted from this obligation. Sixteen articles of the decree detailed the administration of military training and selection (by lot) that would take place under it.[31]

The draft debate provides an excellent expression of the mutually supporting yet diverse views of various liberal factions. For the radicals, *El malacate* erupted against criticism of the draft, wondering when Guatemalans would learn. The rich would always, by whatever unseemly means, think their sons too good, too valuable, for the army: "They consider themselves to be like nobles, like people of different blood." But each citizen had an obligation to the nation, and thus "the denaturalized son, the egotistical man, he who refuses service to the defense, to the advancement of the country, should be cursed. The poor wretches who can scarcely maintain an old and widowed mother by the sweat of their brow have been victimized by the Guatemalan nobles for a long, a very long time; they have been labelled with the epithet of rabble, lower class."[32]

Repeatedly, these people of the lower class, really the salt of the earth, had been called upon to save the country from the messes made by the "nobles." It seemed to the pro-Barrios writer that these men had been treated like slaves. Why, it was asked, should only the poor be forced to make the *contribución de sangre?* The "nobles" had been protected, their status symbolized by the frock coat (*levita*). "The frock coat has been respected because it has been the uniform used by those who feel that they would be dishonored by work, by those who are denigrated by an occupation, by those unfortunates who, useless by any measure, only live in the *tertulias*, on the promenades, at the dances. . . . Frock coats are engaged in endless consumption of liquors; they commit all kinds of crimes." It seemed definite that when these nobles' sons had to march in the ranks, peace would be assured.[33]

During the last half of 1872, the provisional government searched not only for an exemption policy acceptable to the public but also for means to modernize both military and police institutions, which could be used in turn as tools of modernization. New categories were added to the exempt list, such as town councilmen and indispensable artisans. The rules for medical exemptions were tightened and made more specific, requiring infirmities and defects to be visibly "present and permanent." Such firmness seemed reasonable to the government, because "anyone can be exempted from military service by paying a modest compensation fixed by the law; and the [local Political] Chief's prudent judgment can designate to anyone the service compatible with his physical aptitude and the state of his health."[34]

Crepúsculo, expressing the moderate view, attacked opponents of the provisional government who were trying to make the military law odious to the people. The military draft was, it said, a complicated issue, and the regime had reprinted current debates in the French legislature to show just how complicated. If it were a difficult issue in France, why would it not be in Guatemala? The editor noted that among advanced nations only the United States and Great Britain did not have the peacetime draft. Guatemala needed it. "We think the government did what it had to do; but nothing is perfect in human affairs and changes will be made as circumstance shows their need."[35]

A frame for the government's thinking on modernization of the military can be seen in a variety of items published in the *Boletín* at the end of September. It was noted with approval, regarding other Latin American countries, that knighthood in Honduras had been abolished by Celeo Arias, the liberal president of that country who had been propelled into office by a Guatemalan overthrow of conservative president José María Medina. In 1868 Medina had established "the Equestrian Order of Santa Rosa and of Honduran Civilization." To the liberals, that bit of ornamentation seemed just too medieval for a country now involved in building an interoceanic railway. Further afield, an essay commented acidly that a recently failed barracks revolt in Bolivia had been an attempt to re-establish the crazed ways of megalomaniac Gen. Mariano Melgarejo and asserted that "Melgarejism belongs to the past." The notice went on to compare Bolivian changes since the fall of Melgarejo in 1871 with the modernization in Argentina after the 1852 battle of Monte Caseros, which ended the reign of that country's dictator, Juan Manuel Rosas. The notice expressed hope that Bolivia would now abandon anarchy and instead progress as Argentina had done since 1852.[36]

In contrast to the empty pomp in Honduras and barbaric anarchy in Bolivia, a range of practical government efforts had been made to expand literacy in Guatemala through the military, the *Boletín* revealed. The Ministry of War had established a school of military music to correct some remarkable deficiencies at military ceremonies. The school would enroll forty students between ten and eighteen years of age from different parts of the country, pay them two reales per day, and provide daily instruction in vocal and instrumental music, reading, writing, and arithmetic.[37] Simultaneously, and toward the same end, a much more ambitious project was announced. García Granados considered education to be a powerful lever for change, and he wanted it extended to all classes of society. Therefore, basic education would be extended to army personnel in classes required of all soldiers who did not know how to read and write. Reading, writing, arithmetic, and the geography of Central America would be taught. Two separate hours of class would be taught daily by the officer in each unit judged to be best equipped. The officer would receive 10 pesos extra pay per month. Each unit's budget would be increased to meet the expenses of the school.[38] These efforts appear to have been coordinated with plans to establish a military academy to train a modern officer corps. By December

1872, three Spanish army officers arrived to direct the academy. They came upon the request of the Guatemalan minister in Spain that the Spanish government suggest officers for appointment as cadre of the new school.[39]

To strengthen the economy and achieve better use of human resources, the government had a responsibility to foster population growth around the vital ports of San José, Izabal, and Champerico, despite their unfavorable climates. Thus, it announced exemption from the draft for anyone who resided in those towns or who would agree to establish residence there. It is not clear whether this proposal resulted from a reaction against the earlier suggestion to draft soldiers from the lowlands specifically for port duty or from some other cause. It did clearly emphasize the difficulty of maintaining population in the unhealthy coastal area.[40]

Late in October 1872 a legal draft took place, demonstrating how the law would operate in practice. It was done by lot (*sorteo*), and 1,200 men were chosen, with half of the number going to active duty and half to the reserve. Further stabilization was sought through reorganization of the capital's police force into a Guardia Civil — that is, a civil police — organized on military principles of hierarchy. The Guardia Civil would be composed of three hundred soldiers and a full complement of commissioned and noncommissioned officers, with the expectation that this force would provide the security and decorum that society deserved.[41]

Miguel García Granados, having lost his grip on the constitutional assembly by the beginning of 1873, now faced a new round of insurrection in the country at large, beginning with that of Col. Vicente Méndez Cruz, jefe político in Amatitlán. Cruz was easily defeated, but an unending series of insurrections would follow for the rest of García Granados's term of office. For a second time the provisional president himself would take the field against reactionaries in the Oriente, again appointing Rufino Barrios interim president. When he returned wearily to Guatemala City on March 25, it was with the determination to decide finally whether he or Barrios was in charge. He called for presidential elections to be held on April 27. Barrios was easily elected, but resolution of the presidency was not to be decided so neatly. The insurrections had become so threatening — particularly the one organized by Enrique Palacios in Panama, which invaded the Bay Islands and Omoa, Honduras — that Barrios had to take the field against them. His inauguration was delayed until summer (June 4), so García Granados of necessity remained in the office until that date.

When at last Rufino Barrios took over as elected president of Guatemala in the summer of 1873, the establishment of a constitution was still three years distant. His immediate and sometimes brutal executive action made many Guatemalans wish for those protections sometimes called constitutional. Barrios was infuriated by any appearance of resistance to his will, and before the summer was out, he brought the oligarchy residing in Guatemala City to its knees. One prominent citizen, who served as papal consul-general, was imprisoned for weeks without charges. Several prominent merchants were exiled to the provinces under police supervision. Women were reportedly suspended in nets from the ceiling of General Barrios's house. Several men from prominent families were flogged publicly, one dying from the severity of his beating. Another was pilloried for twenty-four hours, then given two hundred palos (lashes) and made to clean the presidential stables. All this activity was so notorious that the British, Italian, and U.S. representatives in Guatemala sent a note to Ramón Rosa, now minister of foreign affairs, asking that he try to mitigate the atrocities. Guatemala now had a president with dictatorial powers who proclaimed himself a liberal. During the dozen years that followed, he would impose a "modern" political economy upon Guatemala that would last until the mid-twentieth century. His methods made him resemble in some ways the literary model, proposed wistfully in Spain, of an iron surgeon who could cut through myriad political obstacles to achieve "progress."[42]

Notes

1. *La república* I, 4 (July 20, 1871), 1. The editorial staff represented supporters of the provisional government who had stayed in Guatemala City during the revolution: Pastor Ospina, Ramón Rosa, Marco A. Soto, Fernando Cruz, and Luís Batres. The first collaborator named was Andres Telles, a close associate of Barrios.

2. Hubert J. Miller, *La iglesia y el estado en tiempo de Justo Rufino Barrios* (Guatemala: Universidad de San Carlos de Guatemala, 1976), 82–90.

3. Redacción, Alcance al *Boletín oficial*, 7 (August 26, 1871). Independence day discourses on politics from the Church hierarchy before and after the revolution emphasized that political liberty required institutional Christianity, cf. Velez, Arroyo.

4. Miller, *La iglesia*, 103–105, 107–108.

5. Miller, *La iglesia*, 117–119, 120; for the role of the juntas patrióticas, see 91, note 44.

6. *Boletín oficial* I, 14 (October 24, 1871).

7. *Boletín oficial* I, 23 (January 3, 1872).

8. *Crepúsculo* I, (January 6, 1872), 1.

9. "Carta," Item #10797, Taracena Flores Collection, Benson Latin American Library, University of Texas, Austin.

10. Mariano Aguilar (Sarjento Mayor) and Mariano Soto (Capitán), San Marcos, 1 febrero 1872, "El tal Furcade," *El malacate* (serie segunda) 43 (February 3, 1872), 3–4.

11. Andrés Telles, "Contestación a una carta firmada R. Furcade, Cura de Mazatenango," *El malacate* (serie segunda) 44 (February 8, 1872), 1.

12. Miller, *La iglesia*, Chapter 5.

13. Cf. Centenario, *Indice general de las leyes*.

14. Miller, La iglesia, 185–198; "Libertad de consciencia de cultos," Crepúsculo I, 32 (June 15, 1872) 1; *Observaciones* (Guatemala: Abraham Fernandez Padilla, 1872), Taracena Flores Collection.

15. "Libertad absoluta de cultos," *El malacate* 51 (March 8, 1871), 1–3.

16. *El malacate*, 58 (April 11, 1872); *Boletín oficial* I, 30 (March 15, 1872).

17. *La república* I, 1 (July 20, 1871), 1–2.

18. Miguel García Granados, Decreto #38, 11 diciembre 1871, *Boletín oficial* I, 22 (December 11, 1872) called elections for convention delegates; *Crepúsculo* I, 8 (January 6, 1872), 16 (March 2, 1872) 17 (March 9, 1872), and 18 (March 16, 1872). Santacruz Noriega, *Gobierno*, 194–196, describes the political composition of the constituent assembly.

19. "Situación," *Crepúsculo* I, 14 (February 17, 1872), 1.

20. *Boletín oficial* I, 35 (April 4, 1872), 1.

21. *Boletín oficial* I, 36 (April 7, 1872).

22. *Boletín oficial* I, 41 (April 24, 1872).

23. *Boletín oficial* I, 47 (May 1, 1872).

24. "La asamblea constituyente," *Crepúsculo* I, 59 (September 18, 1872), 1.

25. *Ibid.*; Santacruz Noriega, *Gobierno*, 403–404, 409.

26. Antonio Cruz, "Constitución," *El imparcial* I, 17 (November 23, 1872), 1–2.

27. "La clase trabajadora i el partido liberal," *Crepúsculo* I, 66 (October 12, 1872), 1.

28. Santacruz Noriega, *Gobierno*, 409–410; *Boletín oficial* II, 4 (January 3, 1873), 1–2.

29. Antonio G. Saravia, "Fuero de Guerra," *Crepúsculo* I, 3 (November 28, 1871), 1.

30. "Pérdida de vidas," *Crespúsculo* I, 8 (January 6, 1872), 1.

31. J. Rufino Barrios, Decree #66, *Boletín oficial* I, 56 (June 20, 1872).

32. Salvador Martínez Flores, "Contribución de sangre," *El malacate* (serie tercera) 69 (June 12, 1872), 1–2.

33. *Ibid.*

34. Ministerio de Guerra, Circular a los jefes políticos sobre enfermedades que esceptuan del servicio militar, Agosto 15 de 1872, *Boletín oficial* I, 67 (August 20, 1872).

35. "La lei militar," *Crepúsculo* I, 52 (September 4, 1872).

36. "Noticias de Honduras," *Boletín oficial* I, 78 (September 29, 1872), 3; "El melgarejismo es de ayer!" based on essay in *Illimani* (La Paz, June 3, 1871), *Boletín oficial* I, 78 (September 29, 1872), 6.

37. Ministerio de Guerra, Escuela de sustitutos, *Boletín oficial* I, 78 (September 29, 1872), 2.

38. Ministerio de Instrucción Pública, Escuelas de primeras letras in los cuarteles, *Boletín oficial* I, 78 (September 29, 1872), 2.

39. "Instrucción militar," *Boletín oficial* I, 99 (December 16, 1872). "Colegio militar," *Boletín oficial* I, 51 (May 26, 1872), applauded establishment of the military academy, with Prussia as the model! The prestige of Prussian unification of Germany was clearly a factor; the article refers to the "astonishing resurrection" of Germany. "Médicos departamentales," *Crepúsculo* I, 56 (September 7, 1872), 1, notes the effort, apparently unsuccessful, to employ army physicians in the departments as public health personnel.

40. Ministerio de Guerra, Acuerdo exonerando del servicio militar a los radicados o que se rediquen en Izabal, o San José, o Champerico, *Boletín oficial* I, 84 (October 20, 1872).

41. "Ley militar," *Boletín oficial* I, 88 (November 4, 1872), 3; cf. "Servicio militar," *Boletín oficial* I, 94 (November 25, 1872), 2; Ministerio de Gobernación, Creación y reglamento de la Guardia Civil de esta capital, *Boletín oficial* I, 98 (December 12, 1872), 2–4.

42. Corbett to Granville, No. 41, July 6, 1873, FO 15/155, 260–269. For the Spanish model of the Iron Surgeon before and after the 1870s, see Raymond Carr, *Spain, 1808–1975*, 2nd ed. (Oxford: 1982), 171, 526, 531, 567, 574–581.

6

Conclusion

The years 1865–1873 formed a period of transition from the rule of Rafael Carrera to that of Rufino Barrios. Carrera's regime had leaned on Spanish imperial institutions for stability, whereas Barrios stressed modern technology, unrestrained trade, and coercive innovation to achieve "liberal" progress. The changes that occurred under Cerna and García Granados between 1865 and 1873 appear to have been decisive, if sparse. They were difficult to accomplish and subject to constant challenges, from both liberals and conservatives. Nineteenth-century Guatemala seemed to require dictatorship to fix a course. In this, its experience seemed similar to that of Latin America in general, where the frequency of failure of legal succession, resulting in instant constitutional change or in paralysis, favored dictatorship. Only oligarchy, rule by the few, could claim to be more prevalent in the region.[1]

Liberal dictatorship, which forced elites to accept a pattern of modernization, appeared in Latin America with increasing frequency in the late nineteenth century. In a confrontation between deeply conservative cultural elements and socially profound technological change, the liberal dictator grasped power in the name of progress. In Mexico, 1867–1880, a concept of "scientific politics," or "conservative-liberalism," came to support the dictatorship of Porfirio Díaz. In Central America, which had not yet established a dominant liberal tradition, the Guatemalan Revolution of 1871 was the specific event that broke the power of the Roman Catholic Church. With it fell a nexus of conservative elements that had hitherto slowed modernization in Guatemala and on the isthmus as a whole. The most ambitious previous effort to pursue liberalism and modernization had come in the federal experiment for isthmian union after independence from

Spain. In a situation where any union was questionable, the liberals had pushed too hard for modernization in the 1830s, outstripping the understanding and consent of the public.[2]

If liberalism in Central America from the 1820s to the 1850s sometimes operated on a basis of dictatorship, it had no adequate theoretical defense for doing so. In the late 1850s, however, Louis Napoleon Bonaparte provided the example of a popular dictator.[3] Very early, this development captured the intense interest of at least one Central American liberal politician, Gerardo Barrios of El Salvador. A self-taught intellectual, Barrios traveled to Europe and was honored personally by Napoleon III. He implemented a serious and potentially effective liberal reform in El Salvador around 1860. But if he aspired to be or acted as a liberal dictator, he failed on the field of battle. Rafael Carrera, his conservative conqueror, thought the liberal policy of Barrios endangered the Church and Guatemalan independence.

Carrera's Salvadoran victory brought his twenty-five-year dominance in Guatemala to triumphant culmination just a year and a half before his death. The Guatemala City elite had declared Carrera president for life a decade earlier; now it made use of his remaining days to identify him in the public eye as an instrument of God. His chosen successor, the uncharismatic Field Marshal Vicente Cerna, was inaugurated without much difficulty in the weeks following Carrera's death in April 1865.

Ostensibly, Cerna continued Carrera's conservative, Church-oriented regime for the next six years. In fact, however, changes of various sorts altered the regime significantly during Cerna's time in office. One change was a perceived weakening of resolve. Cerna, although a successful and respected general, devout Catholic, and family man, lacked Carrera's personal dynamism. Carrera had taken advice and direction from the Church hierarchy, but that in no way reduced the perception that he was quite dangerous if crossed. Cerna, however, appeared unable to make a decision without assent from the Church. Whereas Carrera had humbled the violently partisan Serapio Cruz in 1863, Cerna would face repeated uprisings by Cruz between 1867 and 1870. Dreams of progress, expressed with restraint under the old caudillo, were spoken with increasing boldness when his shadow passed and Cerna took over.

To the pro-clerical and oligarchic governments of Rafael Carrera and Vicente Cerna, Napoleon III's establishment of an Austrian prince as emperor of Mexico and his apparent elimination of the church-wrecking liberal government of Benito Juárez was nothing short of fascinating. Publications of Guatemala's conservative regime make it abundantly clear that from 1863 to 1866 it used Napoleon's Mexican venture as inspiration and justification for itself — that is, for rule by a paternalistic aristocracy, rule by the best. Guatemalan editorials treated the Mexican empire cautiously, but the journalistic pieces chosen as reprints from Mexico and France were more exuberantly candid.

Under Cerna, 1865–1871, there was frank consensus for progress among liberals and conservatives. The problem was to define progress and to determine what kind of modernization it required. Relatively free debate took place in the national assembly in those years, and the future of Guatemala was publicly discussed. Field Marshal José Víctor Zavala and Miguel García Granados contributed notably to the dialogue, providing extraordinary liberal leadership in this milieu. They faced a ring of conservatives in Guatemala City entrenched not only in power but in a political philosophy constructed from the experience of the early Carrera years and wielded with some skill.

An unending stream of cautionary advice aimed to prevent the small literate elite in the capital and the provinces from being seduced by liberal adventurism. The conservatives remained as fearful in their 1870 writings as they had been in 1840. The lower classes were pictured, with Indians as the frequent stereotype, as immobile yet potentially dangerous. They could be brought along the road of progress only with difficulty and, of course, slowly. If pushed too hard or deprived of familiar institutions, they might again rise in fury. The thoughtless liberal who demanded change in accord with some inappropriate "foreign" ideology was viewed as an abomination.

Unrestrained by modesty, Guatemala City conservatives applied their philosophy to show that since independence Chile and Guatemala had formed a conservative vanguard among Spanish American nations. Leaders of these two countries had been wise enough, went the argument, to re-establish their basic institutions after radicals had disrupted them during the 1820s and 1830s. As a result, by the second generation after independence, both nations enjoyed peace, that rarest of commodities in Latin America. With this view and for purposes of elite discipline, conservatives integrated two concepts: that the tiny elite in Guatemala stood on a slumbering social volcano, the masses; and that in Latin America, domestic peace was indispensable to progressive development.

At least from 1867 the Cerna regime showed itself eager to speak of accommodation, to go beyond references to foreign liberal ideology, to assert and try to demonstrate that its own pursuit of progress was based upon flexible principles. It admitted that time might alter profoundly the structure of Spanish American societies and that immigration might make these countries resemble the United States. However, only after such changes occurred should current institutions be changed in their fundamentals. Demonstrating this hypothesis, the regime acted to bring modernizing change in at least four practical areas: internal transportation, port facilities, domestic commerce, and communication.

The Consulado de Comercio, suppressed by liberals in the 1830s and resurrected under Carrera in the 1840s, was the principal instrument available to improve the road system before 1871. Such improvement was vital to agricultural entrepreneurs attempting to expand coffee production in the provinces during these years. Appropriate transportation improvements would tend to validate the Guatemala City leadership on a national scale. However, funding restrictions under Carrera had caused the consulado to limit itself to improving the condition of the existing road system. Cerna saw the need to expand the system significantly with new routes and eventually sought a European loan to pay for the program.

The government at once announced the wonderful improvements that would result from the loan and make life better for future generations. In 1870 it announced plans for a railroad from Guatemala City to the north Atlantic coast, noting that English engineers were already surveying the route. The project fit well into a conservative regime's attempts to prove to liberal critics that it could serve as an engineer of progress. The fact that the regime had completed a steel wharf at San José in 1868, a facility sought since the 1850s, lent credibility to its claim. Likewise, by 1870 the long-desired, spacious new public market in central Guatemala City was well on its way to completion. Both conservatives (before the revolution) and liberals (afterward) designated the new market a monument to progress and modernization, providing the occasion for articles on modern sanitation and scientific nutrition.

The telegraph was a straw in the wind. Cerna's regime took note of the approach of Atlantic cables connecting Europe and America and saw in them a progressive development with which Guatemala must connect. In May 1868 a private company enfranchised by the government transmitted the first telegraphic message from Guatemala City to Amatitlán, and within a week the government announced plans to extend the line all the way to the coast. Yet the telegraph was not developed to the point of significant service until after the revolution — thus the snide suggestion that the Cerna regime had no idea how to use the telegraph and treated it like a museum object.

Another change introduced by the Cerna regime was a pursuit of "scientific" approaches to government. From beginning to end, its spokesmen promoted statistics as the universal solvent of problems blocking development. Statistics were particularly alluring in the late 1860s because national production and export figures went steadily upward in those years. In typical fashion, an editor exulted over these advances in 1869, seeing them as irrefutable proof of progress. The press called for qualified men to help analyze the statistics and to participate in government discussions to decide how the British loan would be spent, urging that the money must be used for progressive development, not frittered away. Governments had no right to be prodigal — rather, they should motivate citizens to be productive.

In his first term as president (1865–1869), Cerna experienced a minimum of hazards. His principal external threat came from the resurgent and militantly liberal Juárez regime in Mexico. Internally, the Cruz revolt of 1867 established a clear and present danger because of its reputed connections with both Indians and elite politicians. Neither threat amounted to much. Mexico made no overt move against Guatemala, and in the end Cruz was destroyed.

However, Cerna's decision to stand for re-election in early 1869 brought to a head tensions that had developed during his term. Field Marshal Zavala's strong candidacy for the presidency indicated that in 1869, as in 1865, the opposition to Cerna was willing to stand up and be counted. During the rest of 1869, liberals in the assembly, led by García Granados, criticized government actions. In late November 1869, García Granados called for a parliamentary vote of no confidence in Cerna. Though the motion failed, it made clear to the public the existence of strong legitimate opposition to the government. Such overt dissent had not been tolerated by Carrera.

In general, Guatemala's civil process in the countryside was based on elites finessing complaints and suppressing revolts in Indian villages. The rural scene in nineteenth-century Guatemala has been described as a series of expansions of state power and control over the rural population. To modernizers, the instruments of control over the Indians inherited from the Spanish period appeared to be ineffective. But even conservatives of Carrera's strength of conviction seemed more interested in defending the old institutions that manifested that control than in protecting the interests of any specific group of Indian petitioners. Under Cerna, foreigners involved in the coffee expansion received some support from the government in land denunciations and in obtaining forced labor. After the revolution new arrangements were made to the same effect.

The spectacular defeat and death of Serapio Cruz in late January 1870 ended the period of civil process. Cerna took the position that parliamentary opposition in Guatemala City had been conspiring with Cruz and ordered the arrest of three prominent oppositionists, including García Granados. All were sent into exile. In the spring of 1870, Cerna's repression seemed to be working. All was calm, and the propaganda organs of government explained smoothly why repression was the correct policy. The government now moved toward reform of antiquated arrangements that seemed particularly harmful to expansion of the new coffee plantation system — such as the traditional, emphyteutic pattern of land tenure. Cerna also launched a reform of the currency system to purge the country of its mongrel collection of inferior and damaged coins and to switch the basis of coinage from the old Spanish system of reales-pesos to the modern decimal-metric system recently adopted in Europe by international convention.

Beneath its apparent stability, however, the regime's oligarchic base was divided. A sizable faction grew impatient with the languid pace of progress. Jules Rossignon's essays voiced this growing discontent. In one, he enumerated the stranded projects that would have amounted to steps toward progress: the railroad proposal trumpeted the year before but now ignored; an expensive textile factory in Antigua and the miraculous ice machine of Edmund Carré, both on the verge of failure because of indifference; and the telegraph, installed but ignored. He hoped the day was not far distant when Guatemala's rulers would recognize that the best way to peace lay in perfecting agriculture, creating new industries, and "leaving for future generations eternal memories of gratitude."[4] A month later in the same journal, Rossignon's boldness was echoed by the younger generation. Recent university graduates Ramón Rosa and Marco Aurelio Soto made an open and sarcastic attack on the Jesuits for advocating medieval religious fanaticism as an approach to society and for defending even at that late hour the usury law of 1840, which forbade lending money at more than 6 percent interest.

The ninety-day military campaign of the Revolution of 1871 unrolled even as this emboldened debate took place. Sixty-two-year-old Miguel García Granados found those elements he needed and cut the necessary deals in Mexico and Guatemala. With fewer than three hundred men in the field during most of the campaign, he primarily employed guerrilla tactics. The quick success of his efforts against an army numbered in the thousands suggests that the country was ready for a new regime and that there was little active support for Cerna outside of the old oligarchy, itself divided.[5]

After his military trumph, García Granados brought about sweeping reforms. As promised, he convoked a constituent assembly elected on a liberal franchise (with a literacy requirement). He restored civil guarantees, including freedom of the press, although the public's lack of experience with that freedom — it was explained — brought such abuse that the government found it necessary to reimplement some regulation. Within a year, reform of the army had been started, as had establishment of public education. With tax reform, a thorough government accounting system was installed for the first time. Anti-monopolist measures, which first abolished the tobacco *estanco* and later freed *aguardiente* and *chicha* manufactures, utilized careful measures to collect taxes on these items, and revenue increased even during transition to the new system.

What had not been promised but had indeed been accomplished was drastic reform of the status of the Church. In a country that had always known a union of church and state, this was surely the most radical facet of the new regime. The Church had been central to the ideology and arrangements of the conservative era; weakening it and removing it from politics eliminated a number of restraints on modernization. Analysis of this most important cluster of reforms indicates that Rufino Barrios was the driving force behind it and that García Granados had simply acquiesced.

The Church's fall from power was manifested in the constellation of measures directed against it: expulsion of the Jesuits and the Capuchins, followed by suppression of all the orders; nationalization of all monasteries and conversion of many of these buildings into public schools; exile of Archbishop Piñol y Aycinena and of his suffragan bishop; suppression of the tithe; elimination of the usury law limiting loan interest; and unprecedented propaganda favoring freedom of religion in broadsides, other journals, and *Crepúsculo* itself.

Although establishment of public education was important among liberal reforms, efforts for a new constitution and a military draft were perhaps equally so in terms of the modernization of Guatemala. The constitutional convention called by García Granados bore no fruit and must be considered a major failure of his administration. Promises to reform the military had been prominent on the liberals' agenda before the revolution. As soon as this issue could be addressed, about six months after the new government took power, modern recruitment became an active and continuing concern. Among the numerous categories of exemption from the new military draft, the most notable exempted anyone who would pay a fee of 15 pesos. This device was common to many countries in the nineteenth century, and it appears to have been considered a revenue as well as a military measure, with the various kinds of "contributions" a citizen could make to the nation being prominent in the discussion. A general literacy program was planned for the army, and a military academy was established with Spanish cadre to train a modern officer corps.

Indians constituted probably more than half of Guatemala's population, but they were not represented in the government, and most of them were culturally separate from the rest of the population. Their drafting and recruitment into the militia after 1873 would result in significant infiltration of their communities by ladino (Europeanized) culture by the end of the century. At the beginning of the independence era in 1821, the social identities of ladinos and Indians had been blurred. Ladinos in eastern Guatemala were then generally viewed by officials as peasants (campesinos), and so were the Indians of western Guatemala, though a special legal framework existed for the Indians. Two notable phenomena raised the ladinos above the Indians in terms of class: Rafael Carrera, a ladino who started as a leader of Indians as well as of ladinos, ended by placing the ladino class (as farmers and local bureaucrats) distinctly above the Indians; also, the coming of coffee culture not only raised the ladino class but by 1899 had ladinoized (which is to say, Europeanized) a significant part of the Indian population. Again, effective establishment of the militia and new coercive wage-labor devices were crucial in this process.[6]

The Rufino Barrios regime (1873–1885) would represent a truly radical departure for Guatemala, and the differences between the two liberals, García Granados and Barrios, have been rather well recognized. But similarities in the regimes that ended and began in the revolution of 1871, those of Cerna and García Granados, have tended to go unnoticed. In context they were both essentially moderate. Cerna's conservatism allowed some progressive measures that Carrera's did not. García Granados went further in the progressive direction, but — with the notable exception of Church matters — this change was only a matter of degree from actions under Cerna. Even when Church affairs are considered, an area in which García Granados was indeed significantly different from Cerna, the evidence shows that Barrios was the motor of revolution: It was he who kicked the Jesuits out of Quetzaltenango without consulting García Granados, who then had to decide whether to break up the team or support his subordinate. When he chose Barrios, the suppression and confiscation of Church elements followed. Most major modernizing changes after the revolution, such as the military draft, were decreed by Barrios during those brief periods when he substituted as acting president in García Granados's place. The record shows the eight-year interregnum (1865–1873) between Central America's strongest conservative dictator and its strongest liberal dictator in the nineteenth century to have been a modulated period of transition through the moderately conservative Cerna and his fellow oligarch, the less-than-radical García Granados. These caudillos, Cerna and García Granados, served the oligarchy, and an essential issue in the switch from the former to the latter centered on the terms of co-opting a broader membership. The Revolution of 1871 enabled co-option and expanded the elite by opening the door fully to the international coffee culture and all that came with it. It would be Rufino Barrios, as iron surgeon, who would attempt to pursue fully the implications of that broader membership — a modern, reconstituted Central America.

Notes

1. The literature on dictatorship and oligarchy is diverse, and I have found the following to be particularly useful: Robert Kern, ed., *The Caciques; Oligarchical Politics and the System of Caciquismo in the Luso-Hispanic World* (Albuquerque; University of New Mexico Press, 1973); Eric R. Wolf and Edward C. Jansen, "Caudillo Politics: A Structural Analysis," *Comparative Studies in Society and History* IX (January 1967), 168–179, especially at 177–178 for summary analysis of the shift from *caudillaje* to dictatorships of "order and progress"; Hugh M. Hamill, Jr., ed., *Dictatorship in Spanish America* (New York: A. A. Knopf, 1965), especially at 35–51; Jacques Lambert, *Latin America, Social Structure and Political Institutions*, Helen Katel, trans. (Berkeley: University of California Press, 1967), 149–166.

2. In the literature, the term "liberal dictator" is established but not common. Cf. Charles Stansifer, "José Santos Zelaya: A New Look at Nicaragua's Liberal Dictatorship," *Revista Interamericana* 7 (Fall 1977), 468–475. The term developed in the Spanish monarchy during the period of military politics, 1840–1868; e.g., Leopoldo O'Donnell should qualify for the title; Bartolemo Espartero, to his left, and Ramón Narváez, to his right, also labeled liberals, are less likely candidates for it.

3. "Bonapartism," in William E. Echard, ed., *Historical Dictionary of the French Second Empire* (Westport, CT: Greenwood Press, 1985), 60–62.

4. J. R. (Jules Rossignon), "De la indiferencia en materia de progreso," *Sociedad económica* II, 17 (March 20, 1871), 129.

5. José Santacruz Noriega, *Gobierno del Capitán General D. Miguel García Granados* (Guatemala: Delgado Impresos, 1979), although documented without citations, was particularly enlightening on the military aspects of the revolution.

6. Carol A. Smith, ed., *Guatemalan Indians and the State* (Austin: University of Texas Press, 1990), chapters 3, 4, 5, 6, and 7.

Bibliography

This study is based upon items listed below and in the notes, especially and more generally upon the Guatemala City journals *La semana* (1865–1870), *La gaceta de Guatemala* (1863–1871), and *El boletín oficial* (1871–1873). Also of general importance were reports from the British legation in Guatemala City, usually by Edwin Corbett, to the Foreign Office (London) during the years 1865–1873. Identification of the many essays of the great Guatemalan writer José Milla (Salomé Jil), at his most productive while serving in Cerna's government, has presented a special problem. In an article on this period published previously (and listed below), I expressed more certainty as to his authorship than I can do now. I have concluded that some items that I believed written by Milla were in fact authored by others. Here I attribute authorship only to signed articles.

Documents and Contemporary Sources

Arroyo, Angel M., presbítero. *Discurso político-religioso pronunciado en . . . el día 15 de setiembre de 1871, en celebración del aniversario L de la independencia nacional.* Guatemala: 1871. Cape Collection, Box 8, Folder 31, Latin American Library, Tulane University.

Casals, Pio (see Palacios, Enrique).

Comité Central Pro Centenario. *Indice General de las leyes emitidas por los gobiernos de la Revolución de 1871.* Guatemala: Comité Central Pro Centario, 1871.

Contreras, Gregorio, and Joaquín Díaz Durán. *Crónicas de la campaña revolucionaria de 1871.* Guatemala: Comité Central pro-Festejos de la Revolución de 1871, 1971.

Estrada Monroy, Agustín, ed. *Datos para la historia de la iglesia en Guatemala.* Tomos II–III, Volumenes XXVII, XXX. Guatemala: Sociedad de Geografía e Historia de Guatemala, Biblioteca "Goathemala," 1974, 1979.

Great Britain. Public Records Office. Foreign Office Section 15 (Guatemala), Volumes 129, 131, 135, 139, 140, 147, 148A, 148B, 151A, 153, 155; Section 39 (Honduras), Volume 35. Microfilm, Bancroft Library, University of California, Berkeley.

Palacios, Enrique. (Pio Casals, pseud.). *Reseña de la situación general de Guatemala, 1863.* Edición, introducción y notas por Jorge Lujan Muñoz. Guatemala: Academia de Geografía e Historia de Guatemala, 1981 (1st ed., 1865).

Piñol y Aycinena, Dr. D. Bernardo. *Constitucionales dogmáticas promulgadas en las sesiones tercera y cuarta del sacrosanto concilio ecuménico del vaticano; pastoral con que las publica en su diócesis, el excmo, é Ilmo. Sr. Arzobispo de Guatemala.* Guatemala: 1871.

Rosa, Ramón. *Semblanza. Arcadio Estrada.* Guatemala: Imprenta de la Paz, 1871.

Salvin, Caroline. *A Pocket Eden: The Guatemala Journals of Caroline Salvin, 1873–1874.* Fiona Mackenzie King, ed., with biographical introduction by Sybil Salvin Rampen; Central American introd. by Wayne M. Clegern. Toronto: unpublished manuscript, 1992.

Solís, Ignacio. *Memorias de la casa de moneda de Guatemala y del desarrollo economico del país,* Tomos I and IIIB. Prologue and notes by Julio Castellanos Cambranes. Guatemala: Ministerio de Finanzas, 1978, 1979.

Telésforo Paúl, S.J., José. *Oración fúnebre del Excelentísimo Sr. Capitán General Don Rafael Carrera.* Guatemala: 1865. Latin American Library, Tulane University.

U.S. National Archives. Department of State. Ministers to Central America. U.S. Archives Microfilms Publications, Film Microcopy 219, Rolls 8, 14, 22, and 23.

Velez, Dr. Don Manuel Francisco, presbítero. *Discurso político-religioso pronunciado en . . . el 15 de septiembre de 1869 XLVIII aniversario de nuestra independencia de la monarquía española.* Guatemala: 1869. Cape Collection (20), Box 8, folder 27, Latin American Library, Tulane University.

Newspapers and Journals

All entries located in the newspaper section of the Biblioteca Nacional, Guatemala City, unless otherwise indicated.

El boletín oficial. I–II, 1871–1873.

El crepúsculo. I, 1871–1873.

La gaceta de Guatemala. XIV–XVII, 1863–1871. Microfilmed from copies in Latin American Library, Tulane University.

El imparcial. 1872.

El malacate. Series 1–3, 1871–1873.

La semana. I–III, 1865–1870. Taracena Flores Collection, Benson Latin American Library, University of Texas, Austin.

Sociedad Económica. I, 1866–1870; II, 1871–1873.

Books

Amurrio, Jesús Julián. *El positivismo en Guatemala*. Guatemala: Editorial Universitaria, 1966.

Burns, E. Bradford. *Eadward Muybridge in Guatemala, 1875: The Photographer as Social Recorder*. Berkeley: University of California Press, 1986.

————. *The Poverty of Progress: Latin America in the Nineteenth Century*. Berkeley: University of California Press, 1980.

Campbell, Stuart L. *The Second Empire Revisited, a Study in French Historiography*. New Brunswick, NJ: Rutgers University Press, 1978.

Cambranes, J. Castellanos. *Coffee and Peasants: The Origins of the Modern Plantation Economy in Guatemala, 1853–1897*. Clara Clason Höök, trans. and ed. Stockholm: SAREC, 1985.

Carr, Raymond. *Spain, 1808–1975*. 2nd ed. Oxford: 1982.

Dougherty, John Edson. "Mexico and Guatemala, 1856–1872: A Case Study of Extra-legal International Relations." Ph.D. dissertation, University of California, Los Angeles, 1969.

Echard, William E., ed. *Historical Dictionary of the French Second Empire, 1852–1870*. Westport, CT: Greenwood Press, 1985.

García Granados, Miguel. *Memorias del General Miguel García Granados*. 4 vols. Guatemala: Ministerio de Educación Pública, 1952.

Gillis, John R. *The Development of European Society, 1770–1870*. New York: Houghton Mifflin, 1977; Lanham, MD: University Press of America, 1983.

Hale, Charles A. *The Transformation of Liberalism in Late Nineteenth-Century Mexico*. Princeton: Princeton University Press, 1989.

Hanna, Alfred J. and Kathryn A. *Napoleon III and Mexico: American Triumph Over Monarchy*. Chapel Hill: University of North Carolina Press, [1971].

Hernández de León, F. *El libro de efemérides, capítulos de la historia de la América Central*. Guatemala: 1930.

López Vallecillos, Italo. *Gerardo Barrios y su tiempo*. 2 vols. San Salvador: Ministerio de Educación, 1967.

Lewis, Gordon K. *Main Currents in Caribbean Thought: The Historical Evolution of Caribbean Society in Its Ideological Aspects 1492–1900*. Baltimore: Johns Hopkins University Press, 1983.

Love, Joseph L., and Nils Jacobsen, eds. *Guiding the Invisible Hand; Economic Liberalism and the State in Latin American History*. New York: Praeger Publishers, 1988.

McCreery, David. *Development and the State in Reforma Guatemala, 1871–1885*. Athens, OH: Ohio University Center for International Studies, 1983.

Marroquín Rojas, Clemente. *Francisco Morazán y Rafael Carrera.* Guatemala: Imprenta Marroquín Hermanos, 1965.

Miller, Hubert J. *La iglesia y el estado en tiempo de Justo Rufino Barrios.* Jorge Lujan Muñoz, trans. Guatemala: Universidad de San Carlos de Guatemala, 1976.

Payne, Walter A. *A Central American Historian, José Milla (1822–1882).* Gainesville: University of Florida Press, 1957.

Salazar, Ramón. *Tiempo viejo, recuerdos de mi juventud.* 2nd ed. Guatemala: Ministerio de Educación Pública, 1957 (1896).

Santacruz Noriega, José. *Gobierno del Capitán General D. Miguel García Granados.* Guatemala: Delgado, 1979.

Skinner-Klee, Jorge. *Revolución y Derecho; una investigación sobre el problema de la revolución en el derecho guatemalteco.* Guatemala: Seminario de Integración Social Guatemalteca, 1971.

Smith, Carol A., ed. *Guatemalan Indians and the State, 1540 to 1988.* Austin: University of Texas Press, 1990.

Stephens, John L. *Incidents of Travel in Central America, Chiapas, and Yucatán.* 2 vols. New York: Dover Publications, 1969 (unabridged republication of 1841 edition).

Tobar Cruz, Pedro. *Los montañeses.* 2nd ed. Guatemala: Ministerio de Educación Pública, 1959.

Villacorta, J. Antonio. *Historia de la repúblic de Guatemala (1821–1921).* Guatemala: Tercer Centenario de la Introducción de la Imprenta en Guatemala, 1960.

Woodward, Ralph Lee, Jr. *Central America: A Nation Divided.* 2nd ed. New York & Oxford: Oxford University Press, 1985.

———. *Class Privilege and Economic Development; The Consulado de Comercio of Guatemala, 1793–1871.* Chapel Hill: University of North Carolina Press, 1966.

Articles

Arriola, Jorge Luís. "Evolución y revolución en el movimiento liberal de 1871," *Revista alero* IV, 36–50.

Burns, Bradford. "The Intellectual Infrastructure of Modernization in El Salvador, 1870–1900." *The Americas* 61, 3 (January 1985), 57–82.

Clegern, Wayne M. "Transition from Conservatism to Liberalism in Guatemala, 1865–1871," in William S. Coker, ed., *Hispanic-American Essays in Honor of Max Leon Moorhead* (Pensacola: Perdido Bay Press, 1979), 98–110. The Spanish version appeared as "Tránsito de conservatismo a liberalismo en (1865–1871)," *Revista del pensamiento centroamericano* 31, 151 (April–June 1976), 60–65.

Phelan, John L. "Pan-Latinism, French Intervention in Mexico (1861–1867) and the Genesis of the Idea of Latin America." In Juan A. Ortega y Medina, ed., *Conciencia y autenticidad históricas. Mexico. Escritos en homenaje a Edmundo OGorman* (Mexico: UNAM, 1968), 279–298.

Wolf, Eric R., and Edward C. Jansen. "Caudillo Politics: A Structural Analysis." *Comparative Studies in Society and History* IX (January 1967), 168–179.

Woodward, Ralph Lee, Jr. "The Rise and Decline of Liberalism in Central America: Historical Perspectives on the Contemporary Crisis." *Journal of Inter-American Studies and World Affairs* 26 (August 1984), 291–312.

Additional Works

Woodward, Ralph Lee, Jr. *Rafael Carrera and the Emergence of the Republic of Guatemala, 1821–1871.* Athens and London, 1993.

Skinner-Klee, Jorge. "La asamblea constituyente de 1872," *Estudios sociales; revista de ciencias sociales* [Guatemala]. 2 (November, 1970), 33–49.

Index